D1549551

Columbia University

Contributions to Education

Teachers College Series

No. 754

AMS PRESS

NEW YORK

VOCATIONAL GUIDANCE IN CATHOLIC SECONDARY SCHOOLS

A STUDY OF DEVELOPMENT AND PRESENT STATUS

BY

SISTER M. TERESA GERTRUDE MURRAY, O. S. B.

SUBMITTED IN PARTIAL FULFILLMENT OF THE REQUIREMENTS
FOR THE DEGREE OF DOCTOR OF PHILOSOPHY IN THE
FACULTY OF PHILOSOPHY, COLUMBIA UNIVERSITY

Published with the Approval of
Professor Harry D. Kitson, Sponsor

BUREAU OF PUBLICATIONS
TEACHERS COLLEGE, COLUMBIA UNIVERSITY
NEW YORK CITY
1938

Library of Congress Cataloging in Publication Data

Murray, Teresa Gertrude, sister, 1884-
  Vocational guidance in Catholic secondary schools.

  Reprint of the 1938 ed., issued in series: Teachers
College, Columbia University. Contributions to educa-
tion, no. 754.
  Originally presented as the author's thesis, Columbia.
  Bibliography: p.
  1. Personnel service in secondary education.
2. Vocational guidance. 3. Catholic high schools--
United States. I. Title. II. Series: Columbia
University, Teachers College. Contribuitions to educa-
tion, no. 754.
LB1620.5.M84 1972   373.1'4'25   77-177098

ISBN 0-404-55754-6

Nihil Obstat:
  C. J. KANE, Censor Deputatus

Imprimatur:
  ✠ WILLIAM A. GRIFFIN
  Auxiliary Bishop of Newark, N. J.

Newark, May 17, 1938

Reprinted by Special Arrangement with Teachers
College Press, New York, New York

From the edition of 1938, New York
First AMS edition published in 1972
Manufactured in the United States

AMS PRESS, INC.
NEW YORK, N. Y.   10003

PREFACE

THE STUDY herewith presented is the outgrowth of an investigation of the present status of vocational and educational guidance in Catholic high schools. After a cursory view of Saint Benedict's Rule as a fore-shadowing of modern guidance, the development of the guidance idea is traced through Catholic educational literature, over a period of thirty years.

A proper understanding of the scope and trends of Catholic second-ary education is required as a background for present practices in the guidance of students. Since complete statistics and analyses are not in print, it was necessary for the writer to compile the necessary data from original sources. Statistics from public schools are also presented to furnish comparative data. It is felt that comparison with a field having similar problems will afford a stimulus to thinking and planning, and cause the outlines of the present study to appear more clear-cut.

These preliminary chapters form an introduction to the chief part of the study—the investigation of vocational and educational guidance as it exists today in Catholic high schools of the United States. The investigator wished not only to present a picture of present condi-tions but also to check the facts obtained against earlier data on guid-ance in Catholic high schools supplied in the White House Confer-ence Report—Education and Training—Subcommittee on Vocational Guidance (1932).

This study presents a picture of present strength and weakness, and indicates trends and tendencies. It is hoped that it will stimulate the inception of programs of guidance suited to size and conditions of the schools. Already the questionnaire used by the investigator has served as propaganda, and as a suggestion of possible techniques for those not already familiar with them. It is hoped also that this study will assist persons who are preparing to do work of an administrative and super-visory nature in education, and will suggest modification of present educational training courses, or inclusion of new courses to meet the need. Diocesan Boards and Superintendents may obtain suggestions and directions from material included. It is hoped that this study will serve these and other educational purposes for educators whose interest has already been expressed in responding to the questionnaires, and has served as a stimulus to the completion of this study.

The investigator takes this opportunity to thank Reverend Mother Monica for permission to continue graduate studies.

To Dr. Harry D. Kitson, Professor of Education in Teachers College, Columbia University, and to the members of the Supervising Committee, Dr. William C. Bagley and Dr. Edward H. Reisner, the writer offers sincere gratitude for advice and assistance rendered.

To the Assistant Director of the Department of Education of the National Catholic Welfare Conference, Mr. James E. Cummings, to the Librarian, Miss Agnes Collins, and to Miss Emma Kammerer, thanks are rendered for valuable personal assistance, most graciously rendered.

Mr. Emery Foster, Chief Statistician in the Office of Education, Department of the Interior, Dr. W. H. Gaumnitz and Dr. Walter Greenleaf, specialists in the same Office of Education, generously devoted time and offered suggestions, for which the writer is very grateful.

To Miss Mary C. Powers, words cannot convey appreciation and gratitude for generosity in time and effort expended.

Finally, most grateful thanks are offered to school officials responding to the questionnaires, to members of the Benedictine Community, and to family and friends without whose assistance this study could not have been completed.

To all who co-operated in any way, sincere gratitude is rendered.

M.T.G.M.

CONTENTS

CONTENTS

FIGURES AND TABLES

VOCATIONAL GUIDANCE
IN CATHOLIC SECONDARY SCHOOLS

A STUDY OF
DEVELOPMENT AND PRESENT STATUS

PROLOGUE

NEW LIGHT ON THE SITUATION

Announcer: The sketch we are about to present takes us into an average American home, where parents are co-operative, but do not always hear directly from school officers just what the school is attempting to do for their children. Such parents know only what their children tell them in the comments upon daily happenings, and consequently have only the interpretations of students, sometimes straight, and sometimes on the bias.

The characters in our story today are a mother, Mrs. Thomas Burns, her sophomore son, Robert, aged 15, and his uncle, David Burns, who is an executive in the City School System. The setting, as we have said, is an average American home. The time: 5:30 p.m.

(A ring of the doorbell, and sound of the door opening.)

Uncle David: (cordially, and warmly) Hello there, Sister-in-law! I was over in this section of the city and thought I'd drop in.

Mrs. Burns: (in a surprised, pleased tone, mingled with relief) Well, David Burns, you surely are welcome. Tom and I are always glad to see you, and today you're a lifesaver!

Uncle David: You're right, and my stomach is the hole in the center!

Mrs. Burns: Tom will be in any minute now. Dinner is ready, and fortunately we have some things to eat that you specially like!

Uncle David: That's fine, and I'll surely do justice to them. But why call me a lifesaver?

Mrs. Burns: Well, you're in school work, and I don't always understand everything they do in schools today. Robert came home a while ago furious because the vocational counselor told him in an interview that he wasn't living up to his capacity, and that it was absolutely necessary for him to do so. He studies the things he likes and lets the others go. History he reads constantly and can't get enough of it—but languages! He merely attends classes—says languages are for girls! He's up in his room now, storming about the new vocational counselor who has just come to the school.

I

Uncle David: Let me have him alone after dinner. But here comes Tom!

Mrs. Burns: (looking out of window) Yes, here he is! (Goes to foot of stairway.) I must call Robert. Robert! Father is here. Uncle David is here, too. Come to dinner. Wash quickly and come down!

(Over the radio—*The Announcer:* And how they did justice to that dinner! Mother and Uncle David were wise enough to say nothing that would bring up school and an explosion!)

Uncle David: Robert, what is this new history book you have?

Robert: Come on up to my room and I'll show it to you! But say, Uncle David, you're in school work—what is this new vocational counselor we've annexed over at our high school? Some nosy woman to mind our affairs for us!

Uncle David: How's that? What's she been saying to you? But first, what's her name?

Robert: Miss Light.

Uncle David: Miss Light!

Robert: Do you know her?

Uncle David: I certainly do. No one does better work than she does. What did she say to you?

Robert: Told me I'm not living up to my capacity! What business is it of hers? It's nothing out of her pocket!

Uncle David: Wait a minute! I can't take these stairs so fast after such a dinner! Now let's see the book!

Robert: It's a dandy. Boy, look at those pictures, will you!

Uncle David: This is fine!

Robert: History is the only study worth while! I get the best marks of the class in history!

Uncle David: What about the marks in other subjects? Or better, how much have you learned in the others?

Robert: Not very much! But say, where did they get this new vocational counseling anyway! They must sit up nights trying to make the students miserable. You didn't have counseling, grandfather didn't have it, and I don't see that you lost out by not having it!

Uncle David: I wish I had had it—I might have made some different decisions in my life! My father didn't need it so much, that's true. There was such abundance in his early years that work was looking for people —not people for work! He had the whole range of occupations to choose from. Have you?

Robert: No, I don't suppose I have. I haven't been thinking much of what I want to do when I get out of school.

Uncle David: But that's why you need vocational guidance. You should look forward and plan to get ahead. Study yourself and study occupations to find a meeting place. I can't like a nephew who isn't ambitious!

Robert: Sure I want to be a success, but I can't see any use in this new stuff!

Uncle David: (interrupting) Where do you get "this *new* stuff"? It isn't new. I thought you read history!

Robert: (disgusted, but surprised—disgust apparent in the way he says "vocational guidance") History! What has history to do with this vocational guidance?

Uncle David: Let me tell you! You know Plato?

Robert: Sure I do. Here he is in this new book—he lived in the fifth century before Christ!

Uncle David: Well, he wrote this statement in planning the model state, in his book, *The Republic:* "There are diversities of nature among us which are adapted to different occupations."

Robert: That's the very thing Miss Light said to me today—and Plato said that?

Uncle David: And that isn't all he said. He insisted that people with superior talent, whether rich or poor, should be trained as leaders—for where will a republic be if it does not have brainy leaders? He didn't mean just people who have talent, but those who have it and use it!

Robert: That's true too—it's one thing to have it, and another to use it!

Uncle David: But we have no record that the Greeks put into effect this recommendation of Plato's. It was in the twilight of the Roman Empire that vocational guidance took on a somewhat organized form. Rome's luxury and vice, you remember, made the people soft and weak. Benedict of Nursia, a little town northeast of Rome, was sent to Rome for higher education. He was disgusted with the way Roman boys acted. He wanted to make something of his life.

Robert: Yes, I read that he slipped away from his sister and their guardian and stayed alone on the mountain for three years. I'll tell you that was something to do! But why did he do it?

Uncle David: For the same reason, I suppose, that you and I go off alone when we want to think out a plan or a problem. Men in near-by places noticed how different he was from others, and came to him to be taught.

Robert: But what has all that to do with vocational guidance?

Uncle David: Benedict developed a plan, after he had labored with hundreds of men. Nobles brought him their sons to educate. After almost a half-century of work, the men in his monastery, as he called it, begged him to write out plans and considerations he had found successful to aid them in carrying on, so he wrote what he called his "Rule," about 540 A.D. Can't you just see him talking it over with the leaders of his group?

Fade-out

(If staged, the monks should be arranged around a T-shaped table, with St. Benedict in the center of the "T," and the Novice Master at the upstage end of the same table. Deans and others, arranged around table, with profile to audience. The monks may wear bachelor's gowns, and cowl, all of black. St. Benedict with long, white beard, bald on top with fringe of hair around head. Porter—old. Others not particularly young, but not old—must be active appearing. The two scenes—this with St. Benedict and the later schoolteachers' meeting might be arranged with identical tables, the Principal seated in school meeting where St. Benedict was seated, and the Counselor where the Novice Master was. Others profile. Very little furniture on stage. None in St. Benedict's scene. Three-section bookcase with books, and a filing cabinet, and classical picture on the wall—or picture of ship, in high school scene. St. Benedict's scene might be to right of stage, and high school scene, left. In St. Benedict's scene, manuscripts in the hands of the men are necessary. A large quill pen and inkpot are on the table, near St. Benedict. When the scene lights up, or the curtains are drawn, all read silently until St. Benedict speaks.)

If on the Radio—*The Announcer:* We see St. Benedict with ten men around the table, each with his manuscript unrolled, reading.

Benedict: Since you have asked directions for a planned life, that all religious homes shall be well and prudently governed, thus shall we begin: (reading from ms.) "Listen, O my son, to the precepts of thy master and incline the ear of thy heart and cheerfully receive and faithfully execute the admonitions of thy loving Father, that by the toil of obedience thou mayest return to Him from whom by the sloth of disobedience thou hadst gone away. To thee, therefore, my speech is now directed, who giving up thy own will, takest up the strong and most excellent arms of obedience, to do battle for Christ the Lord, the true King. In the first place, beg of Him by most earnest prayer that He perfect whatever good thou dost begin, in order that He who now hath been pleased to count us in the number of His children, need never be grieved at our evil deeds. For we ought at all times to serve Him with the good things which He hath given us."

(speaking) This then, is our purpose, that men may realize the gifts that

God has given to them, and realizing, develop *all* to their fullest extent, not with a selfish, proud end in view, but with full responsibility for these talents He has given us, and using all in loyal, loving adoration of the God Who made us."

Valentinian (Dean): You speak truly, for what Roman is there worthy of the name who has not learned obedience? Conquering self is more than all Rome's mighty conquests, and the obedient man is a true conqueror, who fears neither jealousy nor loss of power or prestige.

Benedict: First, my brethren, we shall take thought for admitting new men to our number, suggesting the ways and means we have found from experience are best for those living here, and for those newly coming. We have asked that 'a senior be appointed' who shall counsel and guide new men until they learn to guide themselves in the ways of our common life. The senior, it is understood, is one experienced in the knowledge of men's characters, as well as in teaching perfect ways by word and example. The Novice Master, we have called this counselor, who shall assist each newcomer to study himself as well as occupations to learn wherein he can render greatest service and be happy. Constantine, we have entrusted you with this responsible office, and you have served well for many years. What have you to offer which we have overlooked in writing?

Constantine: In all appointments in this matter the wisdom of the Spirit has been shown. The year of trial for a novice is most wise; the reading of this "Rule" to him three times in that year has due regard for the forgetfulness of youth, and barbarian men, that they may truly understand the requirements and conditions of life here. Each one knows that he is free to depart at any time, and that we may send him away if his life proves not congenial or satisfactory to us.

Benedict: In practice does this prove all that is necessary?

Constantine: So far as Religious life is concerned, yes; that is, for our common life and prayer, both individual and for the group. Our hardest tasks are found in adjusting novices to work that they will do. Publius, our newest novice, being nobly born, resents doing work which he thinks belongs to slaves. Some novices at present in the Novitiate belong, he thinks, to the serving class, and he cannot see why we ask him to do the work they do.

Benedict: Holy Scripture saith that there is no respect of persons before God. Our problem is twofold, therefore; to show to men that all labor ennobles, and to teach them the infinite worth of the individual. Hold *these* before the eyes of Novices—as other Chapters in this "Rule" emphasize just these views of life. Only thus shall we remake society and restore all things in the peace of Christ. Now, Honoratus, have we well defined the duties of the cellarer, or steward?

Honoratus: Most wisely, so it seems to me—for these plans are long-tried-out, and proved. The listing of the tools and the equipment of the monastery is most wise. Only in writing is an accounting accurately committed, so that it may be continuous. The plans for food, for clothing, for sleeping, for serving are most fatherly. The steward has most call to be 'a wise man, of settled habits, temperate and frugal, not conceited, irritable, resentful, sluggish, or wasteful, who may be as a father to the whole brotherhood,' as you have written.

Benedict: And you, Simplicius, what of the Porter's vocation? Can we add anything to what is written?

Simplicius: (with twinkling eyes, and a smile, showing a sense of humor) You must have called upon your experience when you wrote: "Let a wise old man be placed at the door of the monastery, one who knoweth how to take and to give an answer, and whose mature age doth not permit him to stray about." These words amply define the requirements and conditions of the porter's work. Perchance sometimes, a younger Brother may be needed to go on errands, but I see that you have arranged for that also. There is nothing, then, that I can add.

Benedict: Honoratus, what further can you add regarding the artists of the monastery?

Honoratus: Your admonition is sorely needed, that artists be humble. It is more true when a *little* skill has been achieved. When perfection of work has been achieved care for perfection replaces the self-complacency of the early achievements. Concerning those who direct the work there must be even more humility and patience to draw from each newcomer his talent, and achieve his full perfection. We have work of every kind, from simple tasks to those requiring much talent and experience, as well as many skills. In some men the desire to accomplish certain works runs before the talent to accomplish them; then must the director show the novice work that is allied to that which he wishes, and which will use the novice's talent to his capacity. In all this proving of talents, patience and humility must flower in each day's training of the novice. I can add nothing further.

Benedict: When we wrote 'Artist,' it was intended to include all work: in the knowledge of the soil and crops, flowers and animals; in the infirmary with the sick, as well as with stained glass and metal work, with craftsman's work in gold and silver for the vessels of the Altar. We are all artists in God's work, and must see our mission in this light. And the Deans? (turning to them) What have we omitted from the regulations for your work?

Valentinian: I can add nothing, my Father, for you have emphasized co-operation, intriguing men to study, read, and improve themselves so that society may be the better for it; their example and its influence cannot be too highly commended.

Another Dean: The punishment for faults too shows knowledge of men's needs. If a Brother, having failed—as we all do at times—is not willing to amend his fault, social pressure is brought to bear upon him in isolation, refusing him the company of his brethren at table and at prayer. It is most wise, and particularly so because it is not bitter, but kindly. I say kindly, for you have charged the Deans to talk with him, showing him his fault and attitude in the light of another's viewpoint. This individual counseling is most helpful to him and to society.

Benedict: It is in the matter of the Abbot, or Father of the Monastery that we must make most demands; as the Abbot is, so is the Monastery! He must make no distinction of person with the Brothers; must mingle gentleness with severity; must always esteem the welfare of all souls committed to his care, and be to them a Father. He has men of all dispositions and occupations, of all degrees of civilization and social levels, of all ages.

Maurus: Father Abbot, in reading your plan or "Rule" I have rejoiced and have been impressed with the esteem you have for younger men. Rome has held only older men and their opinions in esteem. When you have asked for a council on weighty matters you have ordered that the young speak first. This is not clinging always to the old way, but suggests a readiness to listen to new plans, so long as they are wise; so you will cultivate in young men the desire to think, since they know their ideas will be thoughtfully received and weighed. Youth's thoughts are often wise, and should be taken into consideration.

Benedict: Yes, the Father of the Monastery must be all things to all men; but "he must not be over-anxious, exacting and headstrong, jealous, or suspicious; he must, in all his commands, be cautious and considerate; he must know that it becometh him better to serve than to rule." Let him always use the discretion that shows him loving to all his Brothers.

3rd Dean: But why, our Father Abbot, have you left so much to the discretion of the Abbot? It is in his power, by your "Rule," that he may adjust things at his will. Will all Abbots have the wisdom and the experience you have shown? Would it not be better if you simply stated the plan which you have found most wise, and let that stand?

Benedict: But times and conditions will change, and what serves now will not always serve well in custom and practice. We have ordered then that all changes may be made by the Monastery Head with prudence and consideration for all concerned, and with due discussion. This adjustment to new times and new conditions is most necessary in all times.

4th Dean: Our Father, in this your wisdom has been shown—not only in the writing of this "Rule," but in practice, as we older men have long observed.

Benedict: Then this shall stand as our "Rule" and direction for a simple, prudent, well-ordered life dedicated to God, and tending to realize in each one his greatest possibilities. Let the talent of all be guided into the right channels and be developed to its fullest, that so we may thank God for these talents which He has given us.

(Fading for radio; curtain for stage presentation)

Robert: How modern that all sounds! You say that that was in 540 A.D.? Why that was 1400 years ago!

Uncle David: But wisdom and prudence know no age; they belong to all times. And so you see the plan, founded in the spirit of democracy upon the ruins of class distinctions and the decay of the spirit of privilege. This plan retrieved European lands for civilization! North and west the thousands of Benedictine monks spread, teaching to barbarians the works and arts of civilization. Then in a circular motion, monks from England came to the continent, to Germany and central European lands, until each country of Europe knew their teaching and their culture. So we say that wisdom and prudence know no age, for they are ageless.

(Fading in radio sketch; curtain in stage production)

Lights on School Scene

Announcer: We see now a faculty meeting in Robert's high school, the Principal presiding. (The scene is set in exactly the same manner as for St. Benedict and his monks. Principal presiding.)

Head of English Department: The students are asking why Miss Light has come and what her work will be in vocational guidance.

Principal: I think the Counselor can outline briefly for you what she is here to do.

Miss Light: The Counselor's work is greatly varied, but the sum and substance of it is, she has come to serve—serve faculty and serve students. She must co-ordinate the work of subject teachers, for they must direct their subject matter, while she must watch the interests of each individual student. She must stand ready to consult with each student whenever he so desires, and call for interviews those who do not come, and who do not realize that they have problems. She must therefore be a close student of human nature, of sociology or the science of men living together. She must know working conditions, occupations and their trends, their requirements—their educational requirements as well as others. She therefore must know schools and colleges in their offerings and the record of their graduates—

Grumpy Man Teacher: (interrupting) You have a life-sized program mapped out there. Do you think you can do it all?

Miss Light: Not without your help—teachers, class advisers, and home-room teachers! I shall learn to know the students quickly if you will help me. Can you suggest any burning problem for me now?

Woman Teacher: I'd like to have your help with Robert Burns; he's a bright student, but studies only history, nothing else; he attends language classes, and gives no trouble, but does no work.

Miss Light: I had a talk with him this afternoon. Another teacher had told me the same thing. I think he rather resented my suggestion that he live up to his capacity. I believe he has not seen the relation of languages to history—perhaps that is the difficulty. And he has no idea of an occupation or anything in the future. What is his physical condition?

Principal: Our physical director is here, and perhaps can answer that for you.

Physical Director: Robert's physical condition is splendid in every way!

Miss Light: What of home conditions? I have not yet called at the home.

Teacher (who had proposed Robert's name): You will have splendid co-operation from his home, and his Uncle David is in the School System, and will lend you all aid. I feel that all Robert needs is to see himself as we see him, and that we want him to develop to his full stature and capacity.

Grumpy Man Teacher: Well, our counselor can shed some light on that situation! (general laugh, in which Miss Light joins)

Miss Light: My name always serves for a good laugh, and laughing is a good tonic. I'm most grateful for your help on Robert. With your help, I will do all I can to solve his problem, and those of other students.

(Fading in radio sketch; curtain in stage production)

Robert: Well, I've learned more tonight than I've ever learned before! Those people at school are trying to make me work for myself so I'll be intelligently happy. What a fool I was about the "nosiness" of Miss Light. I'm going to co-operate! And why didn't I see that we couldn't have history without languages! Boy, I'm going to give those teachers the surprise of their lives. I've been asleep and without a thought of the future!

CURTAIN.

... ... paint on that
(stage direction) ... in which Miss Light joins.)

... gain. My name always serves for a good laugh, and laughing is a
good tonic. I'm most grateful for your help on Robert. With your help,
I will do all I can to solve his problem, and those of other students.

(Fading in radio sketch; curtain in stage production.)

Robert. Well, I've learned more tonight than I've ever learned before. Those
people at school are trying to make me work for myself so I'll be intelligently happy. What a fool I was about the "nuances" of Miss Light.
I'm going to co-operate. And why didn't I see that we couldn't have history without languages. Boy, I'm going to give those teachers the surprise
of their lives. I've been asleep and without a thought of the future!

CURTAIN.

CHAPTER I

STATEMENT OF PROBLEM AND
METHOD OF INVESTIGATION

Public High Schools Evolve Guidance Practice

SINCE its inception in 1908, vocational guidance has shown gradual but constant growth in the public high schools of the United States. *The White House Conference Report on Vocational Guidance* in 1932 [1]* showed that more than half of the cities with over 25,000 population made some provision for vocational guidance of students in public secondary schools. This report also showed some activity on the part of Catholic educators, responses having been received from twelve dioceses relative to guidance in Catholic secondary schools.

Vocational Guidance in Catholic Schools

Catholic secondary schools have increased in number and in enrollment until the schools number more than 2,000 and the students more than 270,000. The classes in Religion and religious exercises care for the moral and religious factors which so strongly influence the lives of adolescents. But a consideration of the problem of vocational guidance immediately suggested the following questions:

I. How representative is this presentation of Catholic secondary schools in the White House Conference Report?
   A. To what extent are Catholic educators aware of the problem of vocational guidance?
      1. Does Catholic educational literature shed any light on this question?
      2. Do Catholic colleges and universities offer facilities for training counselors, and teachers with a guidance viewpoint?
      3. What agencies, if any, are assisting in the dissemination of the guidance idea?
II. What is the scope and trend of Catholic secondary education? Comparatively, what is the scope and trend of public secondary education?

* Figures in brackets refer to items in Bibliography.

III. How extensively do Catholic high schools provide for the guidance of their students in the choice of lifework?

What is done to assist them to understand the talents, capacities, and abilities which have been given to them, and how and where those particular talents and capacities may be used to greatest advantage for society and for greatest satisfaction to themselves?

A. Are there studies of vocational guidance offerings in Catholic high schools?
   1. Do other educational studies made in Catholic high schools show evidence of vocational guidance?

B. Are Catholic secondary school officers interested in vocational guidance?
   1. Are they sufficiently interested to make provision for it in schools?
   2. Is this provision on an informal or on an organized basis?
   3. How recently was this work inaugurated?
   4. In what year of school was the work begun, and why was this year chosen?
   5. Was work begun on an informal basis or with a class organized; if begun on an informal basis, has change been made to an organized basis?
   6. Were all teachers used in beginning guidance, or home-room, or selected teachers?
   7. Has time given to guidance been increased, and why?

C. What devices and techniques have been used to accomplish guidance and what devices are now being used, including measurement?
   1. In particular, is a class in Occupations (under any name) offered?
   2. Is it required of students?
   3. Do they receive credit for it?
   4. In what year of school is it offered? Has there been a change in the year, and why?
   5. What texts, or reference materials are used?
   6. Are all occupations presented in the class, or only local ones?

D. How is the guidance program administered?
   1. By the principal or some other school officer? Or
   2. Does the school have a counselor? More than one?
   3. Are counselors Members of Religious Communities?
   4. How much of the counselor's time is devoted to guidance?
   5. Has the counselor received special training for counseling, where?
   6. What relation does the counselor have to deans, class advisers, et al.?
   7. Does the counselor have interviews with students, and how often?

8. Are students' records kept and centralized for use by all teachers?
9. Do students receive educational guidance in high school, and for higher education?
10. Do counselors make placements and follow-up students placed?
11. Does the counselor maintain contact with alumni or alumnae?
   E. For occupational information are there surveys of local occupations? Made by whom? What agencies co-operated? Do reports of surveys come to the counselor's office?
   F. Are alumni, parents, and others organized to assist in the guidance of students?
IV. Is guidance thought of as continuous, and necessitating a technique of discovering and evaluating data on any prospective vocation? What provision is made in the program for acquiring this technique?

Methods of Investigation

Three methods of investigation were employed—historical, statistical, and questionnaire.

In 1934 a questionnaire incorporating most of the questions presented above was sent to educators known to be interested in vocational guidance. Announcement was made that the investigator was undertaking a survey of Catholic secondary schools of the United States with enrollment of twenty-five or more students. A request was made for criticisms, restatements, deletions, or additions. Many of the suggestions were incorporated. The questionnaire was printed and forwarded to secondary schools listed by Diocesan Superintendents, or in the Directory of Catholic Colleges and Schools, 1932-33, published by the Department of Education, National Catholic Welfare Conference.

Steps in the Assembling of Data

To assemble data considered necessary for this investigation, the writer planned and accomplished the following action:
1. Reviewed Catholic educational literature, as shown in Chapter II.
2. Reviewed studies in education which show evidence of vocational guidance in Catholic secondary schools, the result being presented in Chapter III.
3. Reviewed studies in education which present evidence of vocational guidance in public schools of the United States, results being used for comparison.
4. Analyzed Catholic secondary school statistics for 1932 and 1930 to gain

a comprehensive and detailed knowledge of basic conditions, presented in Chapter IV.

5. Analyzed public secondary school statistics to secure comparable data. These analyses (in 4 and 5) were undertaken to answer the following questions on Catholic secondary schools—all shown in Chapter IV:

What percentage are boys', girls', and coeducational schools?

What types do they present—central, parochial or private—and what terminology is used?

What is their distribution in rural sections and in urban, and for the urban, how large are the cities?

What is the distribution in various sections of the United States?

What is the distribution as to size of student body?

How do public and Catholic secondary schools compare as to size and distribution?

What standards are maintained, as shown by accreditation of schools?

6. Sent letters to 105 Diocesan Superintendents and School Officers, requesting permission to forward questionnaires to Catholic secondary schools under their supervision. Eighty-five Dioceses co-operated.

7. Sent questionnaires to 1,648 Catholic secondary schools with 25 or more students throughout the United States, to secure data on present practices and programs of vocational guidance. All states are represented in the 1,004 questionnaires returned by officials of high schools with enrollment of 25 to 2,970—a 61% return.

8. Tabulated the returns on the 33 items of the questionnaire, results being presented in Chapter V.

9. Sent questionnaires containing four items to 65 Catholic colleges and universities, which offer courses in education, to discover the offering of courses in vocational guidance, or courses including vocational guidance, in order to determine facilities for training counselors under Catholic auspices. Request was made for catalog or bulletin to check the content of these courses—with 100% return. Reviewed these catalogs for direct evidence of courses in vocational guidance and tabulated the results shown in Chapter VII.

10. Formulated recommendations for Catholic educators in planning or introducing an organized form of vocational guidance in Catholic schools, as found in Chapter VIII.

Diocesan Superintendents were petitioned in November and December 1934, and questionnaires were sent to secondary schools, to colleges and universities, December 1934 to March 1935. A copy of the college questionnaire may be found in Chapter VII, and the secondary school questionnaire in the Appendix.

CHAPTER II

VOCATIONAL GUIDANCE AS PORTRAYED IN CATHOLIC EDUCATIONAL LITERATURE

Evidence of Catholic Educators' Alertness to Guidance Problems

THAT Catholic educators are alert to the need for guidance is shown in the literature of Catholic education. This literature consists of:

1. Bulletins of the National Catholic Education Association—the general educational association—and proceedings of its annual conventions.
2. Reports of the semiannual meetings of Diocesan Superintendents of Schools.
3. Proceedings of educational conventions of individual Religious Communities.
4. Proceedings of State and Diocesan Conferences of Catholic educators.
5. Proceedings of other conventions which include education in the agenda.
6. Periodicals devoted to education, or which include educational matters.

The National Catholic Education Association is the national and annual gathering for the discussion of all matters pertaining to education. Divisions include the College and University department; Secondary School department, including a Vocational-Counsel section; Elementary Education; Blind and Deaf departments; Seminary Section. Addresses cover all phases of educational interests, problems and new movements, evaluate these movements, and measure them against existing conditions; discussions, both planned and free, permit play of opinion and experience, an application to differing conditions in various parts of the United States, and a "thrashing out" of problems that is most valuable. The *Proceedings* and Bulletins, therefore, may be said to represent the thinking of Catholic educators on present problems of education, for one way to discover the thinking of a group is through printed documents of the group. Consequently, the *Proceedings* of the National Catholic Education Association are used as the criterion.

Historical Rise of the National Catholic Education Association

For the data on its early history, we must have recourse to the files of the National Catholic Education Association. The organization had its rise in a meeting of Catholic college educators held in Chicago in April 1899 and annually thereafter. Since the preparatory departments were then a vital part of college life, consideration of their problems formed an integral part of the proceedings from the beginning. In 1903 was launched the general educational association, including all phases of Catholic education. At the meeting in 1903 there were present representatives of the College, the Seminary, and the Deaf-Mute groups, and the desire was expressed to have a secondary school section, and to direct thought of students to their work in life. At that time college preparatory departments represented a major part of Catholic secondary education. Then came the movement for separation to accomplish greater effectiveness on both levels of work. The Seminary Section, was, of course, definitely pointed toward the fostering and training of vocations to the priesthood. To the Deaf-Mute Section was added later the Blind Section. While evidence concerning vocational and educational guidance for the handicapped appears in every yearbook, extended treatment is not given to it in this investigation; mention is merely made that it existed, was organized, and developed new strength each year, both in numbers interested and in techniques employed. The interest in those handicapped by the war added impetus to this phase.

The 1904 *Proceedings* show the Report of the Committee appointed in 1903, relative to Catholic secondary schools. The group consisted of two members of the College Section, from Washington, D.C., and two superintendents of schools, from Philadelphia and from Altoona, Pennsylvania. Resolution VII designated "the secondary school as intended for those not going to college, as well as for those going to college." [2]

Two Viewpoints Relative to Guidance Shown in Considering
Secondary Education

Almost immediately there began discussion of the concomitants of vocational and educational guidance. The review discloses two viewpoints regarding guidance—the marginal viewpoint, concerned with concomitants, and the focal or direct view, related to functions or phases of guidance. The marginal viewpoint will be made clearer by comparison with the hexagon used in vocational guidance literature by Professor H. D. Kitson (3). In this hexagon the whole man and the whole vocation are considered from many angles, physical, social, mental, economic, moral and physiological. The terms concomitant, marginal, and hexagonal will be used for the one viewpoint; focal, direct, and functional will be used in designating the other.

Guidance Entered the Field of Interest

As was said above, there began almost immediately indications of the concomitants, such as cultural, or leisure-time guidance, health, behavior, personality, clinical and curricular problems, rural life guidance, how to study, guidance of bright students, and educational stimulation. The 1905 *Proceedings* in two papers and discussions touched upon prevocational courses, differentiated courses, educational stimulation, and guidance. Speakers from New York City, Philadelphia, Camden, N.J., and Boston, Mass., urged that the secondary school have two purposes, a preparatory school for college, and a "practical" preparation for those not going to college. "It is a fitting or preparatory school for college; it is a finishing school in which many will get all the higher and humanizing education, that is, all knowledge of history, literature, science they will ever get. Its importance can hardly be exaggerated; if the bulk of our people leave school before they shall have completed this humanizing education we shall ever remain a comparatively unintelligent people." [4]

"Brighter students should be urged to go on in education, and to positions suited to their powers. Its main endeavor [the high school] will be to impart such instruction, partly culturing, partly technical, as will best fit the pupil for early grappling with fate. I merely wish to lay emphasis on the fact that, if we look closely at the conditions surrounding our Catholic people today, the office of high school education would seem to be to provide what is narrowly called a "practical" education for a large proportion of the alumni of our parish [elementary] schools. The graduates of the Catholic high schools will doubtless pursue a technical course of some kind in a college or university—will become physicians, lawyers, architects, mechanical, civil, or mining engineers, or chemists. All these the high school courses must bear in mind." [5]

A Differentiated Curriculum Is Proposed

"We must not be satisfied with finishing them up with a little high school knowledge of commercial education; we must have different courses, one leading to higher grades of education, as well as the commercial." [6]

The 1906 and 1907 National Catholic Education *Proceedings* considered curriculum, as well as the physical, moral, and social elements. Rev. Father McDevitt, in speaking of "The Model School Curriculum" said: "I believe in this broader curriculum not only because these branches have an educational value, but because the complex conditions of our modern life, especially in the larger cities, are gradually forcing upon us radical changes in our whole educational system." But he includes music, drawing, and so on, for better work in "bread and butter branches." "How shall we develop subjects symmetrically with due regard for the spiritual, physical, and mental capacity of the child? Fit the curriculum to our children (1) so as to take care of themselves; (2) so that the child who leaves us before graduation may feel that the school has done for him all that it could or should." [7] "How develop the powers that lie dormant within this body?—for education is preparation for complete living. The curriculum has the obligation of teaching religion and allied subjects, then secular branches to make the student a useful and powerful member of the commonwealth." [8]

"Catholic teachers are not unmindful of the worldly interests of their children and there has been much searching of heart to see if, after all, we may not have hindered our children's careers. Conduct is the half of life." [9]

"His [the student's] moral tendencies have to be guided, and the guidance has to be given in the home and then in the school. After that he is an intellectual being, full of intellectual capacities, and these capacities ought to be tenderly watched and cared for. He is a social being, and as such he should be developed and guided." [10]

"But we say that true education is not a mere instruction of the mind, it does not consist merely in bestowing information on the

mind, but its greatest object is the framing of the heart, and the form-
ing of character." [11]

"Health Supervision in the Parochial School," by a Sister Supervisor
of schools for her Community, added the health guidance note.[12]

The 1908 and 1909 *Proceedings* included the School Library in the
plans for guidance. The Seminary Section discussed teaching habits
of study in social and labor problems to aspirants for the priesthood.
The secondary school group, still allied with the college group, discussed "Physical Care of the Child" in its vocational bearing; also vocations to the religious life and the various activities, covering almost
all vocations included in the convent and monastery life. Well-known
educators urged "that there be in high schools differentiation of programs according to the individual child's needs, and tryout and observation to see objectively what he can do"; they urged also further
education for those who have ability, and financial help for students
who need money to secure educational opportunity. Secondary schools
now requested withdrawal from the college group so that their specific
problems might receive more intensive treatment.

Practice Began to Accompany Theory

In the first decade of the century then, educators may be said to have
merely broached the subject of guidance and from a marginal viewpoint, but they had become receptive to differentiated individual work,
and to the general concept of vocational and educational guidance.
Philadelphia is to be credited with the inception of the work through
the two splendid high schools, one for boys and one for girls, which
provided tryout opportunities and thus necessitated vocational guidance. The work was not so well organized as we consider necessary
for guidance today, but the individual might try out his abilities in
the laboratories and shops; placement and employment opportunities
were recorded and some follow-up was done.[13]

Vocational Guidance Received Direct Consideration

The second decade opened with educators hammering out the idea
of vocational guidance, evaluating and applying it. "The Catholic
Graduate in Business Life" and "The Catholic Graduate in Professional Life" were discussed by prominent business and professional

men, showing requirements, powers necessary, and rewards. In this 1910 meeting, Superintendent Boyle of Pittsburgh said: "It seems that in our schools we are bent on making an intellectual aristocracy. . . . One thing, however, is apparent to even a superficial observer—industrial training, in one form or another, has come to stay. Ninety per cent of students will not be professional in character, and why should the sheaves of ninety bow down before the sheaves of ten? Social stratification of America is vertical. It holds out for separate trade and vocational schools which will take the child of school age, determine his vocation, keep him through the elementary and technical school course until he is turned out a finished craftsman." Discussion was most heated. Those who took part represented many educational centers, but only three expressed unfavorable opinions, holding that this plan savored of "making the individual an efficient unit in an economic system." Superintendent Boyle concluded the lengthy discussion with the statement: "It is for you to consider *how* it shall be adopted in schools; it has come to stay." [14]

Mingling of the Focal and Marginal Viewpoints

The 1911 *Proceedings* showed that discussions emphasized sometimes the focal viewpoint and sometimes the concomitants of guidance. Topics treated included: "Training Girls for Home-Making"; "Aims and Purposes of Catholic Secondary Education—Cultural and Vocational"; "Teaching Pupils How to Study"; "Retardation of Pupils—Differing Criteria"; "Our Children and Their Lifework." The Report of the Committee on High School covered matters of curriculum and of increasing the number of those aspiring to higher education by burses and scholarships. Brother Bede of Danvers, Mass., showed the dissemination of Professor Frank Parson's idea by presenting experiences of various Massachusetts high schools, and the types of work into which students had been forced by hampering restrictions imposed by labor unions; stressed the need of training for character, and urged inculcation of habits of industry and rearrangement of courses of study for preparing better the student going into industry, and not going to college. He showed that discussion had aroused such interest in his home city that one manufacturing company had allowed use of its shops because it was impossible for the school to equip shops.[15]

Chicago was represented in the discussion with a modern technique of analyzing alumni and urged a broadening of vocational choices through occupational information. [16]

Spiritual Values Must Permeate and Motivate Thought and Action

Brother Luke Joseph of Kansas City, Missouri, showed his Community to be earnestly "career-minded" for their students. "Every system of education must take into account not alone with what it deals, but for what it fashions. The life of the child must, then, be viewed from the double aspect of his temporal well-being and his eternal happiness. He must be educated for this world and the next, his powers so developed as to harmonize things of time and those of eternity." "The enlightened teacher will realize that all he possesses of personality, of knowledge and zeal, of study and labor and method are all too meager to meet the full requirements of his work. Hence he will be prayerful. He will find time amid his many and exacting duties to speak individually to his pupils. Since true success in life consists in the courageous performance of daily duty through high motives, the teacher's part in the preparation of the child for his lifework may be narrowed down to the development of two educative elements; first, the principle of purpose in life; second, the art of painstaking labor."[17] In this 1911 Convention, Brother Luke Joseph recalled the fact that eighteen years before, Brother Azarias had said to educators: "There are Catholic boys who were obliged to quit school at an early age for the workshop and factory and who with riper years and larger experience feel the necessity of making up for early deficiencies. What accommodations have we for this class?" "The youth just freed from restraints of childhood, takes upon himself the duties and responsibilities of the man. He has just reached the period in life when he stands most in need of our sympathy, encouragement, and direction." [17]

Brother Marcellinus also emphasized the follow-up idea: "You may ask what teachers have to do with those who have left school? They have much, very much, to do if they would finish the work they began. . . . There are various ways which might be mentioned, for instance by keeping in touch with his occupation, his amusements, hopes and projects, by advising, restraining, encouraging him as occasion requires. . . . You must make the opportunity." [16]

Review of the Vocational Guidance Movement

The National Catholic Education Association *Proceedings* for 1912, 1913, and 1914 discussed guidance from the functional or focal viewpoint. Interest of St. Louis University in the guidance movement was reflected in two papers given by Rev. Albert Muntsch, S.J., of that University; the first in 1913, a résumé of all effort and literature on the vocational guidance movement; and the second in 1914 on the relation of vocational courses. [19:23] The Associate Superintendent of the New York Archdiocese treated also of guidance. [20] Discussion by Brother Joseph Matthew of the Christian Brothers' College, St. Louis, indicated that his Community was alive to the necessity for training the Brothers to meet vocational needs of students. He urged the life-career motive not only through school subjects but also through tryouts, for which the Brothers' schools provided. [21] It is not certain whether Boston or St. Louis should be credited with the second step toward guidance in Catholic Schools. Certainly St. Louis has been most zealous and ingenious.

Concomitants of Vocational Guidance

Brother Constantius of Memphis, Tenn., in 1913 emphasized self-activity of the student: "Persuade him that he has ability and he will labor to justify your opinion of him; but if the master discourage him he loses self-confidence and ceases to make effort. Nothing can be done for a pupil but through him; his self-activity must be aroused, and his interests must be stimulated." [22]

In 1915 Rev. Myles A. McLaughlin, of Boston College, talked on Factors in Prevocational Training and showed a tendency still to fear the cultural neglect in vocational emphasis. [24] The same year "A Taste for Reading—Its Function in the Development of Character" and "The Development of Catholic Secondary Education in United States" took note of intensive and extensive guidance work. [25]

In 1917 National Catholic Education Association *Proceedings*, "Testing the Teacher's Efficiency," "Prevocational Training," and "Keeping in Touch with Educational Movements" showed the awakening of many parts of the country to the vocational theme. [26] This year-book also emphasized the guidance theme in seminary work. Rev. Henry Spalding, S.J., Chicago, said: "It has ever been a pedagogical principle of the teaching Communities of the Church to study a member's talents, and not only to permit, but to see to it that he makes the best use of those special gifts which God in His providence has given him." [27]

Enter Case Studies and Rural Problems

Discussions in 1917 brought out case studies as a method of guidance, and also the rural problem. Rev. J. W. McGuire of Bourbonnais, Ill., showed the guidance movement as comparatively modern, growing out of the exigencies of modern, industrial and social conditions. "The impetus has come from sociologists and social reformers rather than from educators and is derived from a sense of the need of adjustment of our educational system to changing economic conditions." He then cited two typical cases which became public charges due to lack of guidance. "Cases of this kind are the result of social maladjustment and would never have taken place had these unfortunate children received any proper instruction regarding their fitness and qualifications for certain occupations. Advocates of guidance do not claim it will solve all problems of life or of vocations. Most of the favorable literature is unfortunately inspirational, not scientific." [28] Discussion by the Superintendent of Hartford Diocese, Connecticut, showed guidance being given in the schools, though not yet so well organized as is desired, because of financial and staff problems. [29] Brother Bede, Danvers, Mass., wished a wider acquaintance with occupations on the part of the student. "Even in those schools in which the attendance is made up of children from the farms, the trend of the curriculum is away from farm interests, as shown by the silence more or less complete on agricultural affairs and rural betterment. The learned professions are the goal toward which by textbook and precept, the child is directed, but of farming and kindred interests he hears scarcely a word." [30]

The Universities Introduce Guidance Matter

By 1918 there is definite evidence of the inclusion of guidance in the educational courses in St. Louis University, Catholic University,

Washington, and Notre Dame University, Indiana, though these were not differentiated courses. A Master's thesis and one Ph.D. dissertation at Catholic University testify to interest. [31] The 1918 National Catholic Education Association *Proceedings* treated extensively the junior high school, a guidance device. Dr. Dillon, Superintendent Diocesan Schools, Newark, N.J., urged "that choice of vocation be not made too early and hastily." His grasp of the varying levels of ability is most noteworthy. [32]

The following addresses were made to bear directly upon guidance: "Some Modern Fallacies in Education"; "The Psychology of Habit"; "Training Children to Study." [33:34:35]

Various States Further Guidance

Brother Joseph Gallagher of St. James Boys' High School, San Francisco, explained the "Organization of Our Educational Work," showing difficulties surmounted in the desire for complete guidance work. [36] San Francisco lays claim to fourth rank in beginning guidance on an organized plan. New Orleans also had begun in quite a virile way, not only to master techniques of guidance, but also to assemble occupational information. [38]

The 1919 National Catholic Education Association *Proceedings* showed Ohio leaping ahead in grasp of guidance as well as in guidance activities. Visual education, clubs and other extracurricular activities valuable for guidance, and self-government are touched upon from the practical and experiential points of view. [37] "Entrance Requirements for Junior High School" presupposed the "pupil thoroughly acquainted with the idea of educational and vocational guidance." This would seem to indicate that the idea was full grown in these localities. [39]

Diocesan Bureaus of Guidance Are Suggested

Rev. John O'Grady of Catholic University gave in his "Vocational Advisement" the keynote for the succeeding decade. As a practical measure he advocated the adoption in Catholic dioceses of a bureau of vocational advisement. Testing, placement, vocational tryouts, evening vocational classes, adequate and cumulative records, all are urged upon pastors as definitely necessary measures. Brother Thomas of Baltimore substantiated the measures advocated, by case studies. [40]

Guidance and Its Concomitants Intermingled

In 1920 the National Catholic Education Association Convention considered "Religious Vocations for Teaching Orders," "Physical Training," and the "Rural Problem in Guidance." Advisement for occupation for the Negro, the blind, and the deaf-mute received considerable emphasis. [41]

In 1921, some of the subjects treated were: "Vocations to the Teaching Brotherhoods," "Education for Character Formation," "Problems of Motivation," and "High Schools for Negro Catholics." [42] The 1922 discussions were occupied with "Aims and Purposes in Teaching Religion" as bearing upon character formation and life habits, "Thinking Power in Children," and "Tests and Testing." [43]

The necessity for knowing students' home backgrounds and for cooperation between home and school were treated in 1923. "The Teacher as a Social Worker," and "General Principles of the Catholic High School Curriculum" showed an evaluation of guidance as done by public schools and Young Men's Christian Association with a consequent desire for guidance in Catholic schools before pupils left the elementary school. [44]

School Administration and Guidance in the Elementary Schools

The 1924 Convention gave much attention to vocational guidance: "Reform of the Curriculum," "The Superintendent and the Curriculum," "Importance of Health Education and the Superintendent's Responsibility in this Field," and "The Superintendent's Part in the Formation of Religious Vocations," all treat of administrative matters related to the guidance program. [45] "Vocational Guidance in the Grades" warned against too early choice of vocation, and against the adviser's choosing a vocation for the child. "The aim of vocational guidance is not to choose a vocation for the child or to place him in a walk of life, but to study what he is best fitted for by inclination and possibility, and to open a way for him to reach his highest efficiency. Two things minister directly to this end—occupational information and mental measurement. It is obvious that a knowledge of the occupations of the Community is the natural starting point for effective counsel." [46]

Phases of Guidance Discussed

"Social Studies as Preparation for Leadership" dealt with the problem of the gifted. [47]

"The School Library as an Educational Agency"; "Usefulness of Educational Tests" and "Educational Measurements for the Sightless"; "Adjustment of the High School to Present-Day Needs": "Necessity and Scope of Health Education in the Schools"; and "Seed Time for Social Service" add various emphases to phases of guidance. [48]

Marked Interest in Functions and Phases of Guidance

With the beginning of the second quarter of the century there was a marked spurt of interest, activity, organization, and extension in the training of counselors; and records of experiments, dissertations, and studies in many fields of guidance appeared. The *Proceedings* of the National Catholic Education Association were not our only criterion now, for there were added reports of Benedictine, Franciscan, and Capuchin Educational Conferences; State Catholic Educational Conferences; Rural Life Conference Reports; educational bulletins from Catholic agencies and periodicals; and guidance programs in action in Knights of Columbus work and in the Catholic Boys' Brigade.

Various Concomitants of Guidance Discussed

In the 1925, 1926, 1927, 1928, and 1929 conventions of the National Catholic Education Association, there were many addresses of interest to us because the speakers discussed various concomitants of guidance, but only one address had a focal viewpoint: "Vocational Guidance in the High School," in 1925. [49]

Vocational Guidance Presented from the Viewpoint of Experience

In 1930 Rev. Howard J. Carroll, principal of a high school in Pittsburgh, said: "In view of the complicated and ever-changing conditions of the civilization in which we live, it seems unnecessary to stress the need and the utility of vocational guidance. . . . The Committee on Resolutions of the N.E.A., 1927, recommended 'that educational and vocational guidance be considered a primary obligation of organized education'. . . . I maintain that if the purpose of a school is to supply guidance, there can be no question as to the place in our educational system of that movement which has as its object to get parents, teachers, and child 'to bring to bear on the choice of a vocation organized information and organized common sense'. . . . Teachers trained in vocational work are an asset to any school which undertakes a program of vocational guidance. But this does not mean that a school which does not have a trained faculty member should attempt nothing in the way of guidance. There is no faculty so small that it does not have at least one member sufficiently interested and capable of doing much good." He suggests for the teacher who is beginning counseling the use of standard tests as objective means of knowing students; knowledge of home conditions; observation and field trips; use of sound pictures on vocational topics; and talks by specialists in vocational fields. In concluding he states objectives and results of the plan in operation in his high school, showing that the results more than justified the effort. [50]

Catholic Vocational Counsel Conference Was Formed

In 1930 a Life-Guidance Conference had been formed by some prominent Catholic educators. They requested affiliation with the National Catholic Education Association but the Association's Directors refused it. These educators then requested the Secondary School Department of the Association to open its sessions to the discussion of vocational and educational guidance. These interested educators became the Standing Committee on Vocational Guidance in the Secondary School Department. Out of this new enthusiasm, the Standing Committee on Vocational Guidance evolved the Catholic Vocational-Counsel Conference which functioned with great zeal from 1930 to 1934, and in 1936.

Résumé of Theory and Practice in Vocational Guidance

The attention of all secondary school educators was further directed to vocational guidance through the report in the 1931 Conference given by Rev. Maurice S. Sheehy of the faculty of Catholic University. This report covered all literature on the subject of guidance both from secular and from Catholic educators, legislation, formation of National Vocational Guidance Association, statement of principles, list of periodicals, and an annotated bibliography of books and of tests. This helpful résumé was augmented by "Suggestions for a Curriculum in Vocational Guidance" by Rev. E. Lawrence O'Connell, director of guidance for Pittsburgh, which, in the words of the author, "were enough to enable any Columbus in the sea of vocational guidance to find new worlds for himself." The medical director of the Louisville, Ky., psychological clinic showed the "Results of a Guidance Program as Exemplified in Case Studies." The 1931 Convention heard also a "History of Guidance in Europe" and "A Philosophic Basis for Vocational Counsel." [51]

Direct View of Guidance and Its Functions

To treat briefly but adequately of the report of the Vocational Counsel Section in the 1932 *Proceedings* is impossible. From the standpoint of the contributors and of the topics treated, this yearbook is by far the most important for those interested in guidance. All twelve contributors are well-known educators with experience in the guidance field. The naming of the topics will indicate the range of interests involved: "The Place of Vocational Guidance in the Whole Guidance Program; Ways and Means to Promote It" was presented by Rev. Kilian J. Hennrich, O.M. Cap., director of the Catholic Boys' Brigade of the United States. His long experience with boys and skill in guiding them lends weight to his words. "Ways and Means of Interesting School Executives and Administrators in a Program of Counseling" was the topic of Mrs. Irene H. Sullivan, director of parochial schools for the Vocational Council of Cincinnati. The student counselor at Loyola University, Chicago, treated educational guidance in "Helping the Student to Make the Most Intelligent Transition from High School to College." Rev. E. Lawrence O'Connell, counselor from Pittsburgh, discussed "Counseling on the High School and on the Elementary Levels." Miss Mary P. Corre of the Occupational Research and Counseling Division of the Cincinnati public schools presented "Qualifications and Training for Counselors." H. A. Frommelt of Marquette University treated "The Scope of the High School Guidance Program, and the Dangers of Limiting It to Vocational Guidance." Sister M. Priscilla Freidel whose dissertation on guidance is reviewed in Chapter III, spoke on "The Necessity for Guidance in the Elementary

Grades." Miss Ellamay Horan, professor of education at DePaul University, Chicago, discussed "Testing Measures as an Element in Counseling." Miss Helen M. Ganey, educator, of Chicago, treated "Vocational Testing Materials on the Elementary Level," and Sister Aquinas, O.S.F., of Briar Cliff College, Sioux City, Ia., treated "Testing Materials on the High School Level." Rev. John M. Wolfe, Diocesan Superintendent of Dubuque, Ia., took for his subject, "How to Find and How to Diagnose a Subnormal," and Miss Madeleine Lay, chief of social service in Louisville, Ky., psychological clinic, carried on this subject with "The Problem of Guidance with Subnormals."[52]

The Functions of Vocational Guidance and Educators' Experiences

The 1933 Vocational-Counsel Section of the Secondary Education Department continued the discussion of functions of vocational guidance, and reviewed guidance work in the diocese of Pittsburgh. Examination of the *Proceedings* shows so much material bearing directly on guidance, as well as on extracurricular activities and concomitants of guidance, that only a mention may be made of functions and phases which were discussed. Monsignor John M. Wolfe, superintendent of Dubuque, Ia., archdiocesan schools, discussed "Education, Life, Guidance, and Social Justice" in the light of Pope Pius XI's Encyclical Letter on Social Reconstruction. He does not identify education with guidance, for he says: "Education and guidance must thus be consistently interested in the world and its social forms, because both prepare the young for adequate living and for the use of the tools for making a living." [53]

"Guidance in Relation to Occupational Changes and Leisure Time and Recreation in the Next Decade" was discussed by John J. Treacy, of the guidance department of Marquette University who functions with the Milwaukee Vocational Council. He quotes Aristotle: "The endeavor of Nature is that men may be able not only to engage in business rightly, but also to spend their leisure nobly." In "Guidance and Co-operation with Agencies Other Than the Schools," Rev. Francis J. Gilligan, of St. Paul, confirms the need for co-operation by a statement from Pope Leo XIII, "It is Christian prudence not to repel but rather to be able to enlist the help of all honest men in the pursuit of good

whether individual or social." The work of the Employment Stabili-
zation Research Institute was discussed, and the assistance rendered by
Kiwanis Clubs and Business and Professional Women's Clubs. "Guidance and Placement Bureaus" was the topic of Miss Clara A. Dyer of
DePaul University, Chicago, who said: "Placement Bureaus are a part
of organized vocational guidance and training. . . . They ought to adjust the student to activities which will result in success for him." The
nature and function of placement is discussed first, then typical exam-
ples are given.

The educational counselor at the College of St. Thomas, St. Paul,
Minn., discussed the twofold theme, "An Analysis of Vocational Interests and the Problem of Student Adjustment." He showed the use in
Minnesota of the College Aptitude Test, and the specific means used
in St. Thomas College for study of students' interests. He urged the
need for considering the opinion of the school officer who really knows
the student both within and outside of the school in addition to scores
on tests, saying, "Human nature is too complex to be reduced to an
algebraic formula." [53]

Guidance of Gifted Children

In "Guidance and the Gifted Child," Sister Mary Cecil of the College
of St. Catherine, St. Paul, Minn., said: "Nearly all we know about the
gifted child has been learned through investigations of the past fifteen
years." She discussed various plans adopted relative to gifted children,
outlined positive and negative helpful attitudes, and presented a bibliography to assist persons interested. [53]

Guidance in the Diocese of Pittsburgh

Rev. E. Lawrence O'Connell, director of guidance for the diocese of
Pittsburgh, reported a diocesan survey in arithmetic as a preliminary to
guiding students into proper courses and electives in high schools and
vocational schools. "We are convinced that the best guidance can be
obtained through research. So far the plan has worked, and it has been
very little burden on either teachers, pupils, or schools. The expense
has been negligible and the results certainly justify the effort." [53]
"High School Journalism, and Student Publications," "Training Boys
and Girls for Future Social Life," and "Education of the Will—Build-

ing Character" were discussed in the Secondary Education Department of the 1933 Convention. [53]

The 1934 Meeting an Executive Session

Finances did not permit the usual large attendance of Catholic educators in 1934, and only an executive meeting was planned. Reports of the semiannual meetings of the Diocesan Superintendents were incorporated with the *Proceedings*. The October meeting reported an address by the director of guidance in Pittsburgh diocese on "Vocational Guidance in the Catholic School." [54]

The 1935 Meeting Discusses Phases of Guidance

The curtailed program of 1934 was continued in 1935, but the Superintendents' Section again discussed guidance in "What of the High School?" The conclusion voiced was: "Our constant effort must be to offer through the high school curriculum a balanced, general education modified by adjustment, as far as possible, to the peculiar abilities and interests of the pupil." Follow-up of students going to college formed the theme of "An Appraisal of Our Catholic High Schools." "Psychiatry and the Catholic School" showed the value of staff training for treating individual differences and problems.[55]

The 1936 Convention

In the 1936 convention, the usual program was reëstablished and vocational guidance was the subject of one paper in the Secondary School Department. Rev. H. C. Graham, O.P., in urging the adoption of guidance programs, used as an illustration of possible techniques, the program set up in Fenwick High School, Oak Park, Chicago. The training of the counselor and the keeping of adequate records were emphasized. Discussion hinged on opportunities for obtaining training under Catholic auspices, the relative value of interviews and guidance records, and certain guidance devices which were found most effective. Short reports of guidance programs in action were given by counselors who outlined the size, type and function of the particular school, and local conditions considered by them preliminary to planning such program. [56]

In the College Section one paper was presented, giving retrospective opinions of graduates of Catholic Colleges, relative to their college work and the factors found wanting, in the light of their later experience. Many of the students had mentioned specifically the lack of vocational guidance which seemed to them a necessary part of their education.

Encyclical Letter Defining Vocation

In January 1936, Pope Pius XI addressed a general letter, called an Encyclical Letter, on the Christian Priesthood. His definition of vocation emphasizes will and fitness, interpreted as functioning interest and ability corresponding to the interest, and not the mere subjective feeling sometimes associated with calling or vocation. Student counselors will appreciate the definition. [57]

Review of Community Educational Conferences

At the beginning of this chapter mention was made of the fact that some of the religious educational Communities have annual conferences of Community members or delegates, in which they discuss current problems and movements in education. A review was made of printed proceedings of Benedictine, Franciscan, and Capuchin conferences. All these had discussions and reports of action relative to vocational guidance. Discussions have covered all phases of the subject, experiments have been reported with conclusions evolved, school programs have been discussed, and qualities requisite for counselors.

State and Diocesan Conferences Discussed Guidance

State conferences of Catholic educators were reported from Missouri and Pennsylvania and diocesan conferences from a number of dioceses. All show evidence of interest in vocational guidance, discussions of the subject, and action in urging the adoption of guidance programs. The 1935 meeting of Catholic educators in Pennsylvania heard an address by the Head of the Department of Education, Catholic University, later reprinted in the *Catholic Educational Review,* June 1935. The Missouri Conference also heard in 1935 an address which aroused a great deal of discussion. Although proceedings were not printed, copies of the paper and discussions were forwarded to the writer. Diocesan conferences of educators likewise have discussed guidance and the problems of the Catholic schools in the supplying of the facilities for guidance.

Other Conferences and Organizations Which Included Vocational Guidance

The Catholic Rural Life Conference and the Social Action Convention have both included vocational guidance in the discussions of their annual meetings, likewise the International Federation of Catholic Alumnae. Guidance work is an established part of the work for youth conducted by the Knights of Columbus under their educational program and also by the Catholic Daughters of America. Vocational guidance work is an integral part of the program-in-action of the Catholic Big Brothers and Sisters, Boys' Brigade, and the Catholic Youth Organization and Youth Institute.

Periodicals Interested in Guidance

The Queen's Work, organ of the National Sodality, has urged that a week be devoted to the consideration of vocational guidance in Catholic schools where programs have not yet been inaugurated. Vocational Week reports were made by 516 schools in the years 1931-35. Special library projects and posters, publicity in school papers, addresses by representatives of vocations, round-table and open-forum discussions among students, question boxes, skits, dialogues—all have been used as a means of making students vocation-minded. [58]

At intervals, articles on vocational guidance subjects have been published in the *Catholic Educational Review,* published by the Department of Education, Catholic University; in the *Catholic School Journal,* in *The Queen's Work,* organ of the National Sodality, and in *Catholic School Interests;* in releases from the Press service of the National Catholic Welfare conference; and in articles in diocesan Catholic newspapers. The *Catholic School Journal* for February 1937 is devoted to the subject of vocational guidance.

Summary of Literature on Guidance

As we have seen in the review of the National Catholic Education Association *Proceedings,* 1899-1936, Catholic educational literature testifies to the fact that Catholic educators are alert to the need for guidance. This is further witnessed by religious Community educational conferences, and state and diocesan educational meetings; the agenda of the

Catholic Rural Life Conferences and Social Action Conventions, and by periodicals, one of which has definite propaganda for vocational guidance.

Experience with Vocational Guidance

Superintendent Boyle, now Bishop Boyle of Pittsburgh, had said in 1910: "Education develops out of pedagogical experience and not out of mere discussion." Let us see what pedagogical experience with guidance yielded in the same period. Earlier in this chapter, attention was called to the fact that vocational questions relative to the handicapped had been discussed 1903-36 in the Blind and Deaf Section of the Convention *Proceedings*.

In the first decade of this century, as was shown earlier in the chapter, Philadelphia began the work of guidance in two large high schools, one for boys and one for girls, equipped with laboratories and shops for tryout experiences. Placement and employment were cared for, and some follow-up was done. In presenting the 1912-13 *Proceedings*, the secretary recorded that Boston and St. Louis had begun work in guidance. In 1918 *Proceedings*, San Francisco and New Orleans were recorded as "guidance-minded" and Ohio was shown leaping ahead in guidance activities.

Cincinnati Catholic Schools Participated in Guidance

Parochial schools of Cincinnati co-operated with the Civic and Vocational League, organized in 1915 by the Chamber of Commerce and the public schools. Mrs. Irene M. Sullivan, Teachers College, Cincinnati, is the director for the parochial school section, co-ordinating efforts and activities. Our attention was called to three phases of the work: (1) Grade clubs in all the schools; (2) meetings of the board of directors, that is, officers of each club, or delegates, meeting monthly in a central place to conduct business of general interest, to hear speakers and announcements (which are taken back to individual schools) and to propose questions referred for solution; (grade clubs are thus unified); (3) director's office activities including the arrangement of excursions, and organization and distribution of the new material in educational and vocational guidance. Every phase of mental, spiritual, artistic, civic, and health guidance as well as vocational is covered. Personal contacts are maintained with principals and teachers to expand the work. [52]

Pittsburgh Diocese Organized Guidance

After training its director at Harvard and Notre Dame Universities, Pittsburgh reported inauguration of organized guidance in 1928. Co-operation with the Carnegie Institute of Research and with the Pittsburgh Board of Education resulted in Catholic schools receiving testing, inventory, and record materials for their students. [51]

Various Dioceses Incorporated Guidance

St. Paul, St. Cloud, and Duluth, Minn., Dioceses, because of the interest manifested by the University of Minnesota, are very active, but specific data are not at hand. Dubuque, Ia., Archdiocese reports all high schools doing guidance but not sufficiently organized to include in diocesan reports. This suggests a great need, for records of work must be made. Spokane and Seattle Dioceses and San Francisco Archdiocese are making rapid advances in guidance work, co-operating with state and city bureaus in giving to students the benefit of research accomplished, in addition to bulletins from state and city.

Milwaukee Archdiocese Had Complete Organization

Milwaukee may be credited with the most complete organization of diocesan efforts. A professor of Marquette University has been designated Head or Director of Guidance, with offices in the Diocesan Superintendent's suite. The survey report made by his office says: "Every high school should have at least one member of the faculty specially prepared for the work who will act as vocational counselor to students. Such an adviser must be well informed regarding opportunities which the city offers in the respective occupations, and must know qualifications required of those who plan to take up those vocations." [59] Marquette University has provided courses of training for counselors to facilitate guidance work.

A Five-Year Experiment in an Individual School

The experiment of a Philadelphia high school was recorded in the March 1930 *Catholic School Journal*, by its principal. The first objective was the discovery of teachers fitted for counseling, and the training of these counselors-in-service. Students were divided among teachers, not more than thirty to a teacher, and the first fifteen minutes of the day were given to meetings of students with teacher-counselors. Counseling as well as the gathering of information continued during free periods and after school. Information relative to students was gathered from elementary and high school files, from former teachers, from the student, and from his parents. A cumulative record was thus inaugurated. The teacher-counselor was given the responsibility for knowing all about the student, keeping in close touch with him, encouraging and assisting him. A condition which this school discovered is that home-room teachers who are supposed to do counseling, are not doing it—some not even knowing that they are expected to do it. Assistance to students which should be given by teachers is not being given in many instances.

"With all its defects and problems, this school finds a general improvement in scholarship and discipline, a finer school spirit, more kindly relations between teachers and pupils. After five years the unanimous judgment of the faculty was that counseling works, and is a good thing for all. Our system, with all its defects has proved successful and has won the hearty co-operation and endorsement of the teachers and pupils. The system of counseling we have adopted, namely, of utilizing the services of the entire faculty, is far from perfect. No doubt it could be improved by employing one trained counselor and associating with him only such members of the staff as demonstrate special aptitude for student guidance. It is too serious a matter to be entrusted to the whims and vagaries of every individual teacher. Many difficulties arose when the system of guidance was inaugurated in the school. Only a few teachers entered into the work of counseling with enthusiasm; all were willing to help in the work, but the vast majority showed the lack of training for this special type of education.

"In schools where no special attention is given to guidance, we usually find little interest in it. Though most teachers can be trained to become efficient counselors, it demands hard labor, much time and great patience. It is difficult to see how much progress can be made unless a trained counselor devotes all of his time to the work. Though a few teachers never overcome their dislike for guidance of students, many others become interested when they learn what to demand and how to go about it.

"One feature, and an important one, of student guidance should concern itself with helping every pupil to find that vocation in life for which he is best suited. But this should not be the sole aim of student guidance. There are many matters on which the pupils sorely need information and counsel, and it certainly falls within the scope of the school to furnish such help. In fact, more failures might be averted, and many more who are talented might be stimulated to do better work, if someone in the school took a more personal interest in their welfare.

"If we seek better results, we must draw nearer to the individual pupil, and among other things, we must take into consideration his needs and his capacities. Some will be found to be entirely out of place in high schools, others resist all efforts to help them, but many more could be changed into willing workers, if someone on the teaching staff were to take a personal interest in them. When tempted to condemn those who fail in high school, we would do well to remember the traditional high-school curriculum, from which our Catholic schools have deviated little, was organized for a more select group than that which crowds our corridors today. If we are to get anywhere, we must adapt the course to the capacities of the individual pupils." [60]

Summary

We have seen in this chapter the rise of the vocational guidance idea, first through the concomitants of guidance, illustrated by Dr. H. D. Kitson's hexagon of physical, social, economic, moral, mental, and physiological phases. Using the *Proceedings* of the National Catholic Education Association as the criterion, we have traced the growth of the functional view of guidance from its first mention in 1910 through many discussions, some on the functional side, some from the hexagonal or marginal viewpoint, to the Vocational-Counsel Conference formed in 1930. For four years addresses and discussions covered all phases and functions of guidance up to 1934, when lack of finances forced the discontinuance of general meetings, and the substitution of executive sessions until 1936. We may compare the "feeling" for vocational and educational guidance to yeast, leavening the whole mass, slowly but inevitably. A rapid growth, perhaps, would not have been firm and solid. A return to economic equilibrium may show that the seed of guidance really had germinated, but that financial stress had retarded its growth. This belief is substantiated by the question in the Secondary School Section of the 1934 Convention: "Ways and Means to Finance Our Catholic High Schools under Existing Conditions."

The second quarter of the century gave us many other criteria in the educational conferences of States, of Religious Communities, of the Rural Life Conference, and in periodicals.

During all these years of discussion, teachers had been reading, experimenting, organizing, training counselors in service, battling with problems, securing training in universities, and generally awaking to all functions of guidance, and organizing plans in schools wherever it was possible to do so.

Philadelphia and Boston on the eastern coast and St. Louis in the mid-west were among the first to organize plans for guidance in Catholic high schools. New Orleans in the south, Ohio in the mid-west, and San Francisco on the western coast followed next. Pittsburgh in the east, the Minnesota dioceses, Milwaukee, and the Dubuque, Ia., Archdiocese in the mid-west, and the dioceses of Washington State gradually organized plans for guidance. The outlook is very hopeful. To repeat, the return to economic equilibrium may show the seed has fully germinated.

Various organizations devoted to the interests of youth have incorporated vocational guidance as an integral part of their programs-in-action.

CHAPTER III

PREVIOUS INVESTIGATIONS RELATIVE TO VOCATIONAL GUIDANCE IN CATHOLIC SECONDARY SCHOOLS

Types of Research Presenting Data on Vocational and Educational Guidance

PUBLISHED research involving statistics and information relative to vocational and educational guidance may be classified under two heads: (1) those investigating curricular and extracurricular offerings, administrative practices, and the psychology and sociology of adolescents, and (2) those investigating programs and practices of student guidance in Catholic high schools in chosen areas.

Research in Curriculum Showed Guidance Was Regarded as Incidental

Dr. Carl J. Ryan's thesis on "The Catholic Central High School" showed that in 1926 there were 35 Catholic central high schools in existence in the United States. These schools had been initiated by union of two or more parishes which shared the expense—in place of each parish providing high school education for its children. Central high schools had increased in 1930 to 87 and in 1932 to 215, an increase of 600% in six years.

Dr. Ryan showed that of the 35 in existence in 1926, 20, or 57%, stated some provision was made for guidance; of these, six were coeducational, six were schools for girls, and eight were schools for boys. Two schools reported the presence of an adviser, or counselor, two offered occupation courses, four had talks by business and professional men, who studied aptitudes and had conferences with students, six used only conferences with students, and four offered vocational bearings of subject matter in the classes. Tabulation was made from the original questionnaires. [6]

In the same year, Rev. Anthony J. Chouinard, A.M., investigated the extracurricular activities in 200 Catholic secondary schools. These activities are so bound up with student guidance, that we are interested in reading on page 12, "The benefits accruing from extracurricular activities affect primarily the individual; hence the values of extracurricular activities that are classified as social have to be studied in relation to the individual, testing in what way and to what extent they help to train each future member of society in the habits of correct social behaviour, and of worthy and efficient citizenship." He has classified the values of these activities under four heads: academic, social, religious, and moral. It is noteworthy that one school classified the vocational guidance it offered under "Social Values" since "it brought about contact with business leaders." The investigator was disappointed in the attitudes expressed by many of the 107 school officers who replied regarding extracurricular activities. This attitude, he stated, "appears one of mere toleration—may best be described as one of hesitant encouragement." The educational principles which he saw exemplified in properly conducted extracurricular activities were exactly the ones given as the specific reasons for student guidance. These activities, he said also, "are a training ground for recreative and avocational pursuits which especially today must play a noteworthy part in the life of the average citizen, and should serve to occupy in a useful way the hours of leisure time which are at his disposal as the result of a shortened day and week." [62]

Dr. John R. Hagan's splendid dissertation on Catholic Teachers' Colleges, 1928, showed the need for developing courses which provide teachers with training in individual differences in students, and in methods adapted to these differences. [63]

In 1930 Brother Francis de Sales O'Neill, F.S.C., gave us a survey of "The Catholic High School Curriculum, Its Development and Present Status." All but six states were represented in the tabulation. His report of numbers of students in social studies was most enlightening, but student guidance was listed as an extracurricular activity in 37 schools, 15% of those reporting, and educating 3,284, or 6% of the pupils in schools which answered questionnaires. No mention was made of the school year in which this guidance was given.

The author's research in original sources led him to contrast the offerings of early college preparatory schools for boys with the "richness and variety of curricular offerings in institutions conducted for young ladies, which were far more progressive (1819)." "An examination discloses the presence of many subjects found in the modern high school as well as of many others that have long since been eliminated, and for the restoration of which there is a decided demand at the present time. Departmentalization was introduced as early as 1834."

In concluding, the author stated: "Criticism—of the curriculum—is lack of satisfaction with the present status, not disappointment over progress made. The school is a social institution, and as such, must undergo change. Society demands of the curriculum maker that he be on the alert, adapting old courses and developing new ones to meet needs of changing conditions. In that direction lies progress."[64]

In 1931 Dr. John R. Rooney of the faculty of Catholic University made an examination of the curricular offerings of 283 Catholic high schools. Here, also, although every section of the country is represented, and almost every state, vocational and educational guidance in organized form was recorded in only two high schools, one presenting it in first year, the other in the fourth year. [65]

Curricula in Localized Areas

In 1930 Sister Clarence Friesenhahn, of the Sisters of Divine Providence, San Antonio, reviewed "Catholic Secondary Education in the Province of San Antonio." "Province" is a term used to denote a group of dioceses—a diocese being the territory governed by a bishop —which are geographically contiguous. For the welfare of these dioceses the bishops meet in a conference, with one of their number designated archbishop to head such a conference, and co-ordinate its efforts. Six dioceses are comprised in the Province of San Antonio—first, San Antonio itself, Galveston, Corpus Christi, Dallas, Amarillo, and Oklahoma. Eighty-seven Catholic secondary schools were found in this province, most of them small institutions educating from 10 to 250 students. The greater part of the educational effort had come in this century, though 1847 saw the establishment of the first school. Growth has been gradual but constant. Because of distances, almost one-half of the secondary schools were necessarily boarding institutions, and girls exceeded boy students by about 50%. Fifty-four of the 87 were accredited, principally by the state. No student guidance was mentioned, although in regard to social studies these schools were on a par with schools in more populous areas. These social studies might have contained guidance matter, but no mention was made of it. (In the present investigation this absence of guidance is borne out, but a very active interest has been manifested in ways and means for the introduction of guidance in an organized form.) [66]

Brooklyn Diocese Curricula came under the microscope of research of Dr. William P. A. McGuire, S.M., in 1932. Offerings in social science, as in all the foregoing, have been very wide, but vocational guidance was almost negative. (More recently this has been remedied, at least partially.) In concluding, the summary stated: "The high schools of the diocese show the lack of vocational training. Vocational lectures, or an active personnel service, would be a great help in determining the student's future." [67]

Private and Public Secondary Education in Minnesota Compared by Dr. L. V. Koos

Private and Public Secondary Education, by Dr. L. V. Koos, was issued by the University of Chicago Press in 1931. The University of Minnesota sponsored the study, hoping to learn more of secondary schools than can be learned from forms filled out, and cursory supervision. All accredited high schools of the State were reviewed as to student body, achievement, curriculum, and faculty. Catholic high schools, Scandinavian (Lutheran), independent or private-venture schools, and public high schools, large, medium, and small, were examined and results reviewed.

While the study does not present definite guidance matter, several phases of the investigation have a distinct bearing on guidance of students.

As to the curriculum, the author stated on page 162: "The offerings of private schools as a group are unquestionably more traditional and conservative than are those of the public schools. Catholic schools are nearest to the public schools in the matter of the curriculum." Again, on page 198 he mentioned "the appreciably superior intelligence of students in Catholic high schools, at least on the level of the last high school year." His statement on page 197 concerned vocational training rather than guidance, "that larger proportions in Catholic schools plan to continue in other schools, mainly non-collegiate, because of the relative lack of opportunities for occupational training in the schools attended."

The figures presented in the tables must be corrected. First, the figures for the number of schools and students in Catholic secondary schools, 1915 to 1928, are incorrect, the per cent of error running from 24% to 37% in different columns. The table showing enrollment in high schools is also far from correct. Figures have been quoted from the United States Office of Education, 1929, although the bibliography showed familiarity with the 1928 Catholic Directory of Schools and Colleges from the official source of statistics, the Department of Education, National Catholic Welfare Conference. May it be repeated here that the Office of Education, Department of Interior, will hereafter not gather figures of Catholic secondary schools, but accept figures from the Department of Education, National Catholic Welfare Conference, Washington, D. C.

Again, statistics regarding coeducational schools, both in Minnesota and in the United States, do not bear out the statement made in Chapter VII, that "A majority of private schools enroll students of one sex only, whereas all but a small proportion of public schools are coeducational." In 1930, of Minnesota's 66 Catholic high schools, eight were boys' schools, 13 girls' and 45 coeducational, as shown in Table III on page 68 of the present investigation. This same table shows for the United States that Catholic coeducational high schools in 1930 constituted 54.3% of the total.

Regarding accreditation, Dr. Koos stated that many small private schools were eliminated from the study because of non-accreditation. Our 1930 figures show approximately 50% accredited, many small high schools to a minimum of 40 students being included, though Dr. Koos states: "Usually only the larger private schools seek and achieve accreditation, even though the standards applied contain no reference to minimum enrollment" (Chapter VII). Achievements of students in college are quoted from the Association of Colleges and Secondary Schools of Southern States, as well as from Minnesota. Catholic secondary schools of the Southern States are considered not representative of Catholic schools in general. The Southern Association as a standardizing agency has been accomplishing great changes, but these changes were needed most in that section, both in private and in public schools.

While Dr. Koos stated definitely that one reason for his study was "to provide a better understanding of comparative public and private secondary education," a review of the book reveals elements discounted, which, in all fairness, should have been considered. [68]

A Study of the Catholic High School Principal

Because the principal of the high school plays such an important part in the program of guidance, The Catholic High School Principal is of interest. In this book, Dr. Francis J. Crowley, Dean of the Graduate School of St. Louis University, reports an investigation of 243 schools, enrollment being the basis of division into four groups. All sections of the United States were represented. Distribution of the 243 high schools into boys', girls', and coeducational schools was typical of all Catholic high schools at that time. It is most significant that

PROFESSIONAL COURSES OF MOST USE TO PUBLIC AND CATHOLIC HIGH SCHOOL PRINCIPALS

	Koos	Crowley
	Per Cent of H. S. Principals Who Stated These Courses Were of Most Use	
	Public	Catholic
High School Administration..........	61	84
Principles of Secondary Education.....	20	29
Psychology of Adolescence...........	20	25
Educational Measurements...........	18	21
Vocational Guidance................	12	0

	Per Cent of H. S. Principals Who Have Taken Certain Courses	
	Public	Catholic
Principles of Secondary Education.....	66	44
Educational Measurements...........	36	41
Vocational Guidance................	14	4

Size of the 21 Catholic High Schools Which Had Counselors

	Number of Schools	Per Cent of That Class
Schools from 1–100..............	6	4
Schools from 101–250..............	7	11
Schools from 251–500..............	3	14
Schools from 501–1,342............	5	42

21

boys' schools formed an increasing percentage as the enrollment increased. The percentage of girls' high schools was large, but typical of Catholic secondary organization.

In his study of preparation of high school principals and their functions, Dr. Crowley recorded the professional courses of most use to Catholic and public high school principals. Dr. Crowley used Dr. Koos' study of public high school principals in the comparison of professional courses presented on page 44.

Dr. Crowley urged most strongly that, in preparation for their administrative work, principals elect courses that will prepare them for every phase of activity that their duties will require of them, and student guidance is one. Not every principal will act as counselor in his school, but he must be the pivot around which the program will move, and without which proper functioning of guidance is impossible. At all times the principal is most important in the guidance program. [69]

Secondary Education Under the Jesuits in the United States

In 1932 Rev. William J. McGucken, S.J., Ph.D., published the results of his research at the University of Chicago in the Jesuit system of secondary education, under the title, *Jesuit Secondary Education*. The book has much of interest from the practical side as well as the philosophical, in view of the fact that this Religious Community has provided more completely than any other for the guidance of students, particularly through appointment of counselors. On page 231 he quoted from page 52A of the catalog of Boston College High School, 1926: "One of the questions of highest importance to every high school graduate is the wise choice of a profession or vocation according to one's character, talents, and attractions, both natural and supernatural. No student with a serious outlook on life will fail to determine well in advance of his graduation the career which, under God's providence, will best assure his temporal success and his eternal happiness. In this matter the assistance of the Student Counselor will be invaluable. His hours will be arranged to afford ample opportunity of conferring with the students." Similar matter appeared in the Georgetown Preparatory School Catalog, 1926, page 11. The author indicated that a light teaching schedule usually was given to the counselor, and in some cases the counselor was entirely free to confer with students at all times, with a separate office to insure privacy. [70]

In the Jesuit schools, which are always for boys, there is added to the regular classroom staff, one teacher who usually has one or two classes, with the remaining time at the disposal of students. The author stated that school catalogs earlier than the 1890's did not mention such an endeavor, and that it did not become a regular feature of Jesuit administration in the United States until the last decade, the 1920's.

Many of the Jesuit schools replying to questionnaires in this investigation have enclosed printed matter from catalogs or bulletins which indicates the fact that all their schools supply counseling service on an organized basis. The one phase which seemed lacking in many of these schools was provision for information on occupations. [70]

Vocational Guidance from the Student's Own Viewpoint

In the preceding studies quoted, the educator's viewpoint has been expressed. A recent study by Sister M. Mildred Knoebber, O.S.B., *The Self-Revelations of the Adolescent Girl,* quoted the student's most sincere expression of opinion concerning future lifework. Covering, as it did, 30 states and more than 3,000 students, in both public and Catholic high schools, the sampling was wide. No names were signed to questionnaires and the officials of the schools whose students filled out questionnaires did not receive or see what the students had written. Perfect freedom of expression was, therefore, safeguarded.

The investigator stated that the vocational futures of the girls were the subjects of their greatest interest; real anxiety existed in their minds regarding occupations, and they could not see why schools did not provide amply for this most pressing need, at least with information enough to afford some choice of work that they might desire to follow. [71]

The Beginning of Interest in Vocational Guidance in Catholic Secondary Schools

Sister M. Jeannette Roesch, O.S.B., presented the first research in the immediate field of vocational guidance in 1918. [31] On page 63 of *Vocational Guidance of Catholic Youth* she advocated an organized system "necessary to make the guidance of students a success. While every teacher may and should aid in preparing students for their life-work, there should be in every secondary school someone who more particularly devotes his time and energy to the vocational guidance of the students. This is necessary to avoid, on the one hand, duplication of effort, and on the other, partial or complete neglect." On page 54 she stated: "The object sought is that he, the student, direct his work toward a definite aim, for with an end in view he does his work more con-scientiously, more thoroughly, and more willingly than he would other-wise. Work so performed reacts upon him and aids in the formation of character." She desired that all agencies interested in youth collaborate: "If home, school, and church unite their efforts and present to the child the highest ideal as the motive for his lifework, and by systematic training of hand, head, and heart, help him to realize that ideal, the work of development and guidance of vocation shall have been achieved."

"The work of teachers and superintendents will necessarily be in-creased by vocational guidance," the author warned, but of its benefits for the child she stated: "It is about the age of twelve that school and its duties become irksome to the child, and this is the time to place before him for serious consideration the need of preparing for a definite future career. . . . It matters a great deal to convert his objective interest into subjective interest and to convince him that for success in his future work he needs just exactly what the school gives him." "Catholic teachers are willing to make sacrifices and will gladly bear the added burdens if by doing so they can aid the children whom they consider their God-given charges." [31]

White House Conference Report

The White House Conference, Education and Training, Subcom-mittee on Vocational Guidance, in 1932 reported a survey of 72 dio-ceses, 15 of which were quoted as carrying on one or more vocational guidance activities. [1] Three dioceses reported discussion of occupa-tions in regular classes, four published studies of occupations for school use, 12 held group conferences for discussion of occupations or oc-cupational choices; in 11 schools students had individual conferences with counselors, two had organized employment services, nine had ar-

rangements for giving scholarships, one reported fulfillment of the
state recommendations and co-operation with the Junior Employment
Service, while one reported full diocesan organization for high school
students' guidance, and two, discussions of religious vocations. This
Report will be discussed later in this study.

Investigations of Guidance Practices

In 1933 Notre Dame, Fordham, Loyola University in Chicago, and
Villanova College, Pennsylvania, surveyed guidance practices in chosen
areas.

At Notre Dame, Sister Mary Clarice Gansirt, O.P., contacted 274
large high schools enrolling from 150 to 2,000 students; 103 replied.
To the author, the question, "Do you provide vocational guidance for
the students in your school?" connoted the presence of a counselor, so
the specific question, "Do you have a counselor?" was not asked. However, question 22 in Table I, asking if the advisers had been specially
trained, resulted in 27 affirmative answers, although the places of training were not mentioned. Sixty-one of the 103 schools provided vocational guidance, 25 offered separate classes in occupational studies, 64
provided this occupational information through subject-matter classes,
22 kept guidance records of students, 65 offered conferences of counselors with students, 51 offered conferences of counselors with students
seeking work, 77 offered educational guidance, 4 reported the counselor a vocational guidance expert, 38 principals acted as counselors,
while in 27 schools the home-room teacher acted in this capacity. In
11 schools, an instructor not assigned to a home room acted as counselor, and in 12 schools, other school officials, not designated, acted as
counselors. This splendid thesis offered a survey of periodical material
by Catholic educators on guidance, supplied partial and definite guidance programs in effect at that time, indicated attitudes of sympathy
(expressed) with the movement, then turned to specific functions or
services of guidance, particularly counselor's services. Sources of data
for guidance were treated specifically and also the administration of
guidance. Forms and bulletins from large Catholic high schools were
reproduced.

The author suggested three problems for further investigation: the
present status in the smaller high schools; practicability of a diocesan

organization for the supervision of guidance; and feasibility of the school guidance personnel handling placement. [73]

Personal Visitation of Fifty Large High Schools

Sister Mary Priscilla Freidel, S.N.D., reported her findings to Fordham University after personally visiting 50 large Catholic high schools between New York and the Mississippi River—schools which included 15.81% of the Catholic high school population according to the 1930 census. This visiting of schools gave most excellent personal knowledge of them. Regarding guidance practices, she reported that schools in one section did not differ radically from those in another locality. The author reported "noticeably different attitudes displayed towards the guidance movement, depending upon the position of the person interviewed." Principals, in all cases except three, showed less knowledge of the problem of guidance than counselors did. Where an efficient personnel for guidance existed, the principals usually reacted favorably toward the movement. Fifteen boys' schools, eight girls' schools and one coeducational school had guidance personnel—almost 50% of the schools visited. In 20 of these schools, the counselor maintained a separate office. In the schools of one Religious Community, a counselor was provided in every high school, but the types of counseling varied. Four counselors were trained.

The author found greater approval for counselors who had teaching duties. Records in most schools consisted of scholastic marks, given at widely different intervals. Only three maintained guidance records, properly so called. Tryout courses as understood in vocational education were not found in any of the 50 high schools.

In the summary of the chapter on the guidance program, these findings and conclusions were given: "Administrators of schools for boys have provided more adequately for guidance opportunities than was found in girls' schools, the ratio being approximately 2-1. One-half of the schools have some form of guidance, five of the schools having well-developed plans in operation. In 82% of the schools where there was some form of counseling, grades nine to twelve were included in the program. Instructional courses in guidance were offered in six schools only. One-fourth of the administrators considered counseling the most important duty if this was part of the regular teacher's work.

Standardized tests were not favored in the majority of schools, and only six schools used such tests occasionally. Counselors and home-room teachers determined the scope of guidance activities, and only six schools offered courses in vocations. Three schools were found having complete programs of vocational guidance. These schools had counselors, provided opportunity for interviews, conducted classes in occupations, administered intelligence tests, kept records of interviews, character traits and tests, and maintained placement bureaus. In the majority of schools the activities were indefinite—something super-added, but not considered essential, while in some schools assembly talks by school officers or by business and professional persons constituted the entire vocational program. None of the counselors had had experience in vocations, but had theoretical knowledge."

Preparation for college consisted almost entirely of provision for the courses necessary for entrance. As to the counselor, the author stated in her conclusions that "The work of the counselor has not been recognized as a profession separate from teaching." In her recommendations she said: "Flexible programs should be introduced into the high school to meet local needs. It cannot be too strongly recommended that counselors prepare for their important duties by taking professional courses. Only such persons should be selected for the office who possess the power to enrich the lives of youths placed in their charge."

Summarizing, the investigator stated that counseling is the vital phase of any guidance program, and that an effort is being made to give students in Catholic high schools this service. "It is evident from the findings, that counseling on an organized basis is still in its infancy in Catholic secondary schools. The number of activities is extremely limited. This situation emphasizes the necessity for co-ordinating the guidance activities, especially those related directly to the student. It also stresses the need for trained counselors." [73]

A Study of Guidance Practices in Girls' High Schools in Nine Midwestern States

At Loyola University, Chicago, Sister M. Ignata Biehn, S.C.C., in 1933 presented a study of four-year high schools for girls in nine states of the mid-west, where geographical similarity would tend toward similarity in occupational and professional life. Two hundred and twenty-seven schools were sent questionnaires, and 90 or 38.19% replied. Three schools had been discontinued because of finances, one had been transferred to another city, and one stated positively that it was not "guidance-minded," while 32 reported merely that no vocational information was given. Enrollment varied from 100 to 1,100. In all, 24 activities were reported by 90 schools, which led the investigator to state that "guidance is still in the formative period in these schools." Talks by professional persons and vocational information associated with school subjects seemed the most frequently used devices for guidance. Little mention was made of counselors, as home-room teachers seemed to bear the burden of such guidance as was done. Only one school offered credit for guidance work. One school treated the subject for one semester, one for a year, and one for grades 7, 8, and 9 in junior high school. Four said that they offered a course in vocational guidance, calling it "Guidance," another "Vocational Education" and another "Occupations through Problems." Although these offerings were very incomplete, some schools had indicated a very definite interest, hoping "that an entering wedge will soon be made for this much needed work." [74]

Report on Vocational Guidance in Girls' High Schools in Philadelphia

A Master's thesis at Villanova College, offered in 1933 by Sister Irmina Kelly, I.H.M., covered the vocational guidance in girls' high schools in Philadelphia where the investigator was occupied with this work. The growth of this guidance was covered from its inception through the inclusion of the White-Williams Foundation and the appointment of teachers in the schools as counselors. Present practices were described as found in six public and two Catholic high schools for girls. Each school had a full-time executive counselor with separate office, a part-time counselor, a complete set of records, case studies of special problems, and vocational guidance bulletins. In her summary the investigator stated that the work was very valuable, but that much remained to be done; programs were well organized, but that the chief lack was in administration and in co-operation of faculty with counselors. The program had been in effect for four years at the time of the report, and followed the state guidance program.

Summary

Review of previous investigations showed 14 pieces of completed research, nine studies which record Catholic high schools offering guidance, and five which investigated the vocational guidance programs in Catholic high schools. Dr. Crowley's report on the *Catholic High School Principal* showed 21 counselors in 243 schools. He presented for comparison Dr. Koos' study of public high school principals which indicated principals who had had guidance courses and other courses helpful in guidance work. Fourteen per cent of public high school principals and 4% of Catholic high school principals had had guidance courses.

A study of Central Catholic high schools in 1926 showed that 57% made provision for guidance, and approximately 6% had counselors, the boys' schools providing more adequately than the girls' or coeducational schools; 12% had talks from business and professional persons; 12% showed the occupational bearings of high school subjects; 17% used counseling interviews; and 6% offered courses in occupations.

In a review of extracurricular activities, one school of the 200 schools surveyed listed vocational guidance among its offerings. Others of the 200 schools may have offered guidance in subject classes, but made no mention of it.

Two studies of Catholic high school curriculum, one covering 250 schools, the other 283 schools, present a great contrast. In the survey of 250 schools, 15% were found to offer vocational guidance among their extracurricular offerings to 6% of their students; in the other study .75% of schools offered guidance.

One very recent study of adolescent girls revealed real anxiety in the minds of the girls regarding occupations, and showed also that the vocational futures were the subjects of greatest interest to these girls.

Dr. McGucken's study of Jesuit secondary education indicates that the Jesuits have made greater provision than any other Religious Community for guidance of students, since all their schools provide student counselors. Occupational information was not indicated definitely.

Of the five studies on guidance in Catholic schools, one in 1918 related to the necessity for guidance, and the system and work entailed.

The four other studies were samplings. One investigator contacted 274 schools and received 103 replies from schools ranging from 150 to 2,000 students: 59% of the schools offered vocational guidance; 22.3% had separate classes in occupational studies; 62.1% provided this occupational information through subject-matter classes; 21.3% kept guidance records of students; 63.1% had conferences of students with counselors; 50% had conferences of counselors with students seeking work; 74.7% offered educational guidance; counselors were vocational guidance "experts" in 4% of the schools; in 37% of schools the principal acted as counselor; in 26.2% home-room teachers acted as counselors; in 11.6% other school officials not designated by name, acted as counselors.

A second of the four studies surveyed four-year high schools for girls in nine midwestern states; 90 of the 227 schools replied, and these ranged in size from 100 to 1,100. Four and four-tenths per cent offered vocational guidance courses; little mention was made of counselors, as home-room teachers seemed to bear the burden of guidance. In all, 24 activities were found in the 90 schools, which led the investigator to conclude that guidance was still in the formative period in those schools.

A third investigation covered 50 large high schools from the Atlantic coast to the Mississippi River, by personal visitation of the schools. These schools enrolled 15.81% of Catholic high school population according to the 1930 census. Approximately 50% of the schools had guidance personnel, and 40% of the counselors had separate offices; 8% of the counselors had received training; in 82% of the schools there was some form of counseling, and 25% of the administrators considered counseling the most important duty of guidance; 12% had instructional courses in guidance; 12% offered courses in occupations; 12% used standardized tests; 6% maintained full guidance records; approximately 50% had some form of guidance; 10% had well-developed plans and 6% had complete programs of guidance.

The fourth investigation covered six Philadelphia girls' schools, four public and two Catholic schools. Each school had a full-time and a part-time counselor with programs of guidance and bulletins, but the investigator felt that a lack of co-operation between faculty and counselors hindered possible progress. These studies in themselves are an indication of a wholesome interest in vocational guidance.

It is the purpose of the present investigation to add to the information available by investigating on a nation-wide scale, and by discovering latest developments.

Summary of Previous Studies

1918—Catholic University of America	Sr. M. Jeannette Roesch, O.S.B., Ph.D., *Vocational Guidance of Catholic Youth.*
1927—Catholic University of America	Rev. Carl J. Ryan, Ph.D., *The Central Catholic High School.*
1927—Catholic University of America	Rev. Anthony J. Chouinard, A.M., *Extracurricular Activities in Catholic High Schools.*
1928—Catholic University of America	Rev. John R. Hagan, Ph.D., *Catholic Teachers' Colleges.*
1930—Catholic University of America	Brother Francis de Sales O'Neill, F.S.C., Ph.D., *Catholic High School Curriculum.*
1930—Catholic University of America	Sr. M. Clarence Freisenhahn, Ph.D., Div. Prov., *Curricular Offerings of Secondary Schools of the Province of San Antonio.*
1931—Catholic University of America	Rev. John R. Rooney, Ph.D., *Curricular Offerings in 283 Catholic High Schools.*
1931—University of Chicago Press	Dr. L. V. Koos, *Private and Public Secondary Education in Minnesota.*
1932—Catholic University of America	Rev. William P. A. McGuire, Ph.D., *Brooklyn Diocese Curricular Offerings in High Schools.*
1932—University of Chicago	Rev. Wm. J. McGucken, S.J., Ph.D., *Jesuit Secondary Education.*
1933—Notre Dame University	Sr. Mary Claire Gansirt, O.P., Ph.D., *The Status of Vocational Guidance in 274 Large Catholic High Schools.*
1933—Fordham University	Sr. M. Priscilla Freidel, (Notre Dame) Ph.D., *Guidance Practices in 50 Catholic High Schools.*
1933—Villanova College	Sr. M. Irmina Kelly, (I.H.M.) A.M., *A Study of Vocational Guidance in Girls' High Schools in Philadelphia, Pennsylvania.*

1933—Loyola University, Chicago   Sr. M. Ignata Biehn, S.C.C., Ph.D.,
                                     *Vocational Guidance Practices in
                                     Girls' High Schools in Nine States.*
1935—St. Louis University   Sr. M. Mildred Knoebber, O.S.B.,
                                     Ph.D., *The Self-Revelations of an
                                     Adolescent Girl.*
1935—St. Louis University   Dr. Francis J. Crowley, Dean of
                                     Graduate School, St. Louis Uni-
                                     versity, *The Catholic High School
                                     Principal.*

CHAPTER IV

SCOPE AND TRENDS OF CATHOLIC SECONDARY EDUCATION

Understanding Catholic Secondary Schools

BEFORE embarking on our survey of vocational guidance in Catholic secondary schools, it will be necessary to know something of their beginning, and to understand the scope and trends of Catholic secondary education throughout the United States. A knowledge of Catholic secondary schools, their philosophy, organization, objectives, and problems will assist materially in the formation of plans for the future.

Historical Sketch of Colonial and Early Secondary Schools under Catholic Auspices

"The earliest reliable traces of Catholic secondary education in the original colonies are to be found in the Manor Schools established by the Jesuits in Maryland. In his *Catholic Church in Colonial Days*, Dr. J. C. Shea mentions an academy at Calverton Manor conducted by Mr. Ralph Crouch about 1640-50. Traces of a similar institution are found in 1677 at or about Newton Manor under the direction of the Jesuits. In 1746 the Jesuits opened the famous classical academy at Bohemia Manor. . . . The training in all these academies was chiefly classical in character. Coincident with the opening of the Manor schools in Maryland, the Jesuits opened a secondary school in New York in 1682, known as the New York Latin School. . . . Its building stood on the site of the old "Trinity Church" at Broadway and Wall Streets. . . . Long before these schools were established, the Franciscans had done splendid work all along the southern and western coasts. . . . There is reason to question whether any of them ever attained secondary level, although Shea incidentally makes mention of a classical school and preparatory seminary at St. Augustine as early as 1606." [64]

Catholic Secondary Education in the Eighteenth and Early Nineteenth Century

"Catholic secondary education in the early colonies, as was the general practice, was confined exclusively to boys. The Church in America was at that time hampered as far as educational undertakings were concerned, both by dearth of teachers and lack of funds. Moreover, the ideas prevalent during that period were opposed to anything resembling higher education for women. Prior to the beginning of the nineteenth century, only one institution destined exclusively for the higher education of Catholic girls was opened, namely, the Ursuline Academy in New Orleans established in 1727." [64]

"Some profess to see in the school established by Father Richard in Detroit in 1802 the forerunner of the present parish high school. It is certain that the zealous pastor of Detroit actually opened in connection with his parish a high school for boys, and a year or two later a similar institution for girls. So advanced were his educational theories that vocational training especially of an industrial character played a large part in the instruction of his school. His memorial letter to the legislature of Michigan discloses that knitting, sewing, and spinning as well as other features of domestic science were taught along with the regular subjects of study. In accord with his comprehensive plan, schools were established in Detroit, Mackinac, and Monroe." [64]

Church Decrees Which Increased Schools and Supervisory Boards of Education

Not all secondary schools were under Religious Communities, for many were begun by educated Catholic laity. To increase and perfect schools for the rapidly increasing population, the First, Second, and Fourth Provincial Councils of Cincinnati, 1855-1882, [76] and the Second and Third Plenary Councils of Baltimore [77] issued many decrees regarding education. The importance of this question of education and supervision is shown by the fact that in 1884 one-fourth of the decrees enacted by the Third Plenary Council of Baltimore concerned education. These decrees stated the necessity for erecting schools, and establishing superintendents, boards of supervision, and examination of teachers and of students in urban and rural districts. The rise of the diocesan superintendent from school boards has been pictured in a dissertation of 1935, *The Diocesan Superintendent of Schools, A Study of the Historical Development and Functional Status of His Office,* by Rev. John Voelker, Ph.D. of the Catholic University of America. [78]

First Survey of Catholic High Schools

Two researches with their most valuable bibliographies of original sources give a very complete review of the historical rise of Catholic education in the United States. *Principles, Origin and Establishment,* 1908 [79a] and *Growth and Development of the Catholic School System in the United States,* 1912 [79b] by Rev. J. A. Burns, C.S.C., Ph.D., are invaluable for a knowledge of Catholic schools. The second book states on page 363, "The movement for the establishment of high schools in connection with the parish schools has been spontaneous, and first showed itself in the efforts of individual pastors, in widely separated parts of the country, to add high school courses if not a complete high school to the parish school." [79b]

He showed that high schools were of four classes: (1) the college preparatory, which was either the academic department of a college, or a separate institution; (2) the academy, which was usually a private school, independent of the parish; (3) the parochial high school, usually an extension of the parish elementary school; and (4) the central high school. These central high schools had been established either by the diocesan authorities or by the concerted action of two or more parishes. The college preparatory schools and the academies were usually supported by tuition, but the parish high school was usually free to members of the parish, and the central high schools were free to all, in most cases. Of the 310 high schools listed by the Joint Committee on High Schools in 1910, 19 were central. Since Rev. Father Burns' report as Chairman of the Joint Committee on High Schools was the first survey of high schools, it is interesting to note that, exclusive of college preparatory departments, 310 high schools reported in 1910 and more than 100 high schools did not report; 8,212 boys and 6,612 girls, a total of 14,824 were served by these 310 schools responding. One-half of the high schools had four grades, and of the remaining 155, 66 had three years, 60 two years, and 29 one year. Somewhat the same condition existed in the 10,213 public high schools in 1909-1910,

according to the report of the United States Commissioner of Education, for one-third of the schools had a curriculum lasting from one
to three years. According to the *American Catholic Quarterly Review*
of July 1901, there were at that time 90 independent Catholic secondary
schools with an attendance of more than 5,000 students. Rev. Burns
shows that the Catholic Directory, 1910, enumerates 709 Catholic
academies for girls with more than 25,000 students, and points out that
"the number of girls in secondary schools seems to be considerably
greater than that of boys." [79b]

Survey of High Schools Instituted

The work of the Joint Committee on Secondary Schools led the
National Catholic Education Association to make in 1915 a survey of
secondary schools. In 1919 the Department of Education, National
Catholic Welfare Conference, was established, and inaugurated biennial

FIGURE I

GROWTH OF ENROLLMENT IN CATHOLIC HIGH SCHOOLS AND
ACADEMIES, 1915–1934 *

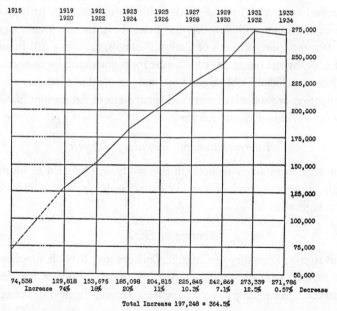

Total Increase 197,248 = 364.5%

* *Reproduced (with additions) from Directory of Catholic Schools and Colleges,
1932–33, Department of Education, National Catholic Welfare Conference.*

surveys of secondary schools. Figures 1 and 2 show the trends of Catholic high schools in respect to schools, faculty, and students.

Sources of Correct and Erroneous Statistics

The Department of Education, National Catholic Welfare Conference, has been and is the only authentic source of data relative to Catholic school statistics. Two other sources are sometimes quoted, but erroneously. The first of these, the Office of Education, Department of the Interior, has found its figures so inaccurate that arrangements have been made to receive correct data from the Department of Education, National Catholic Welfare Conference. The second source is the annual "Official Catholic Directory," whose tabulated statistics have been found very inaccurate, although its records of schools in each diocese, with addresses and officials, are helpful. [80] This statement is not a condemnation, but a plea, for with greater co-operation from dioceses, and keener insight into educational statistics, this Directory might be a source of authentic information gathered annually. Only in a few diocesan reports are statistics so differentiated as to give light on figures at the various levels of school work. This Directory, since its inception early in the nineteenth century, has been the source of much significant data regarding growth of Catholic schools, and may still be made invaluable, by the use of adjusted forms for reports, and by co-operation of diocesan officials. All figures quoted on Catholic schools in this investigation are statistics from the Department of Education, National Catholic Welfare Conference. [81]

Interpretation of Secondary Schools

The term "secondary schools" in this study will be used to mean all schools above the level of the elementary schools, and will include junior high schools.

Sources of Data

The 1932-33 Directory of Catholic Colleges and Schools supplies the latest printed data of specific or detailed matter. Figures for graphs and statistics from 1915 to 1930 have been secured from this Directory, since it is issued by the Department of Education, National Catholic Welfare Conference. [81] This Department has issued later general

FIGURE 2

GROWTH OF CATHOLIC HIGH SCHOOLS AND ACADEMIES, 1915–1934

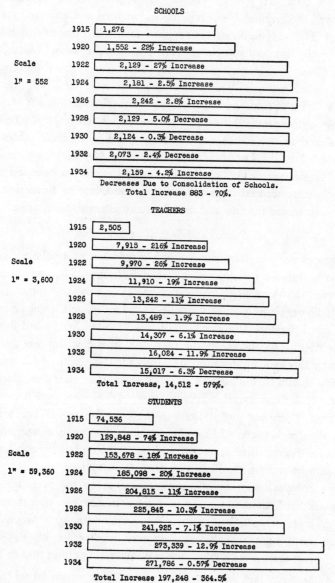

SCHOOLS

	1915	1,276
	1920	1,552 - 22% Increase
Scale	1922	2,129 - 27% Increase
1" = 552	1924	2,181 - 2.5% Increase
	1926	2,242 - 2.8% Increase
	1928	2,129 - 5.0% Decrease
	1930	2,124 - 0.3% Decrease
	1932	2,073 - 2.4% Decrease
	1934	2,159 - 4.2% Increase

Decreases Due to Consolidation of Schools.
Total Increase 883 - 70%.

TEACHERS

	1915	2,505
	1920	7,915 - 216% Increase
Scale	1922	9,970 - 26% Increase
1" = 3,600	1924	11,910 - 19% Increase
	1926	13,242 - 11% Increase
	1928	13,489 - 1.9% Increase
	1930	14,307 - 6.1% Increase
	1932	16,024 - 11.9% Increase
	1934	15,017 - 6.3% Decrease

Total Increase, 14,512 - 579%.

STUDENTS

	1915	74,536
	1920	129,848 - 74% Increase
Scale	1922	153,678 - 18% Increase
1" = 59,360	1924	185,098 - 20% Increase
	1926	204,815 - 11% Increase
	1928	225,845 - 10.3% Increase
	1930	241,925 - 7.1% Increase
	1932	273,339 - 12.9% Increase
	1934	271,786 - 0.57% Decrease

Total Increase 197,248 - 364.5%

Reproduced (with additions) from Directory of Catholic Schools and Colleges, 1932–33, Department of Education, National Catholic Welfare Conference.

figures and statistics in releases to the press and in a pamphlet printed in 1936, but the depression has not permitted publication of detailed data for 1932. To secure them, the investigator visited the office and reviewed the original school reports, and secured and analyzed the statistics. The 1934 figures were supplied to the Department of Education by the diocesan superintendents, presidents of school boards, and chancellors of dioceses. Since they were merely total figures, no analysis was possible. This plan of securing data, paralleling the plan of the Office of Education, Department of the Interior, makes available in the second year of a four-year period, data from original school reports, and in the fourth year, data compiled in diocesan offices and forwarded to the Department of Education, National Catholic Welfare Conference. The comparative statistics for public secondary schools were secured from specialists in the Office of Education, Department of the Interior and from bulletins issued by that office.

Statistics of Secondary Schools

Figures are not complete for either public or Catholic secondary schools. Bulletin 1931, No. 20, Office of Education, Department of the Interior, shows on page 1 a total of 22,237 or 92.9% of the true total. [82] The exact number of Catholic secondary schools is not known.

Table I presents cumulated data for the United States, and then for each state. The diocese is the unit in Catholic school work, consequently diocesan figures must be added for state totals. In a few and minor instances, boundaries of dioceses overlap state boundaries, a necessity for travel and communication. Adjustment had been made for this. There are 105* dioceses in the United States. Nevada, formerly divided between California and Utah dioceses, was erected as a separate diocese three years ago, and has no secondary schools, according to a letter from the Bishop of Reno, January 1935.

For comparative purposes, statistics are given for 1934, 1932, and 1930 for the United States, and then for each state. In 1934 there were 2,159 high schools, an increase of 4.2% over 1932 when there were 2,073 high schools; 1932 showed a decrease of 2.4% over 1930 when there were 2,124. Faculty numbered 15,017 in 1934 or 88.3%

---

* At the close of 1936, the Los Angeles-San Diego Diocese was divided and San Diego Diocese became the 106th in the United States. In tables presented, these dioceses are united, since separate statistics cannot be obtained immediately.

TABLE I

CATHOLIC SECONDARY SCHOOLS—COMPARATIVE STATISTICS FOR 1934, 1932, 1930

States		No. Schools	Faculty			Students			
			Reli-gious	Lay	Total	Boys	Girls	Unclas-sified	Total
Total U. S.	1934......	2,159	13,258	1,759	15,017	118,305	153,481		271,786
	1932......	2,073	15,529	2,495	16,024	117,662	152,632	3,045	273,339
	1930......	2,124	12,217	2,090	14,307	102,060	135,080	4,785	241,925
Alabama	1934......	20	88	12	100	520	564		1,084
	1932......	19	80	7	87	599	544		1,143
	1930......	14	84	5	89	520	520		1,040
Arizona	1934......	6	33	3	36	174	271		445
	1932......	6	38	6	44	275	178		453
	1930......	6	26	9	35	123	176		299
Arkansas	1934......	10	47	3	50	247	405		652
	1932......	10	47	3	50	247	405		652
	1930......	10	43	5	48	222	364		596
California	1934......	94	529	141	670	4,062	6,565		10,627
	1932......	78	596	230	826	4,612	6,738	75	11,425
	1930......	78	526	163	689	3,676	6,159	260	10,095
Colorado	1934......	26	160	6	166	1,035	1,227		2,262
	1932......	16	129	11	140	954	1,087		2,041
	1930......	17	103	17	120	823	1,034		1,857
Connecticut	1934......	13	110	30	140	121	1,314		1,435
	1932......	12	120	30	150	89	1,344		1,433
	1930......	10	85	15	100	159	1,146		1,305
Delaware	1934......	7	21	7	28	253	204		451
	1932......	7	22	8	30	237	304		541
	1930......	8	23	5	28	213	224		437
District of Columbia	1934......	16	128	3	131	678	1,186		1,864
	1932......	16	103	30	133	678	1,196		1,874
	1930......	16	94	21	115	594	1,048		1,642
Florida	1934......	16	90	13	103	451	882		1,333
	1932......	17	90	12	102	452	934		1,386
	1930......	16	76	10	86	428	683		1,111
Georgia	1934......	5	34	...	34	308	290		598
	1932......	5	38	10	48	338	324		662
	1930......	6	35	8	43	396	233		629
Idaho	1934......	7	42	3	45	173	440		613
	1932......	6	36	3	39	147	406		553
	1930......	7	42	5	47	152	375		527
Illinois	1934......	118	1,261	130	1,391	12,134	12,210		24,344
	1932......	122	1,240	215	1,455	10,922	14,667		25,589
	1930......	131	1,103	175	1,278	9,673	13,463	141	23,277
Indiana	1934......	42	277	22	299	2,214	3,036		5,250
	1932......	47	275	25	300	2,147	3,475		5,622
	1930......	47	232	13	245	1,738	2,887	14	4,639

TABLE I, *Continued*

States		No. Schools	Faculty Religious	Lay	Total	Boys	Students Girls	Unclassified	Total
Iowa	1934......	154	504	38	542	3,508	5,043		8,551
	1932......	127	617	56	673	3,998	5,214	215	9,427
	1930......	136	543	54	597	3,303	4,866		8,131
Kansas	1934......	37	171	13	184	1,402	2,019		3,421
	1932......	44	230	25	255	1,487	2,078		3,565
	1930......	45	210	21	231	1,517	2,027		3,544
Kentucky	1934......	57	248	8	256	2,083	3,541		5,624
	1932......	55	258	25	283	1,691	2,854		4,545
	1930......	67	250	20	270	1,358	2,557	30	3,945
Louisiana	1934......	58	315	50	365	2,755	3,102		5,857
	1932......	59	315	37	352	2,652	2,760		5,412
	1930......	60	273	38	311	2,160	2,514		4,674
Maine	1934......	12	63	6	69	636	818		1,454
	1932......	11	74	20	94	674	834		1,508
	1930......	11	58	24	82	429	626		1,055
Maryland	1934......	37	238	7	245	1,198	3,476		4,674
	1932......	34	202	34	236	2,071	1,756		3,827
	1930......	40	211	38	249	1,931	1,780		3,795
Massachusetts	1934......	113	578	13	591	6,182	9,967		16,149
	1932......	111	697	66	763	5,567	9,491	904	15,962
	1930......	97	685	63	748	5,185	8,220	926	14,331
Michigan	1934......	145	767	45	812	8,046	9,276		17,322
	1932......	110	714	85	799	7,000	8,632	71	15,703
	1930......	119	662	55	717	5,693	7,610	341	13,914
Minnesota	1934......	71	371	93	464	3,338	3,685		7,023
	1932......	70	374	99	473	3,440	4,058		7,498
	1930......	66	337	93	430	3,119	3,618	18	6,755
Mississippi	1934......	25	66	2	68	470	595		1,065
	1932......	22	88	3	91	738	567		1,305
	1930......	23	72	7	79	456	618		1,074
Missouri	1934......	59	396	64	460	3,146	4,563		7,709
	1932......	55	421	68	489	3,156	4,658		7,814
	1930......	64	388	65	453	3,119	4,355		7,474
Montana	1934......	16	84	12	96	729	869		1,598
	1932......	11	67	16	83	466	920		1,386
	1930......	12	59	16	75	520	828		1,348
Nebraska	1934......	48	244	14	258	1,187	1,811		2,998
	1932......	48	196	14	210	1,329	1,977		3,306
	1930......	50	179	14	191	1,022	1,879		2,901
Nevada	1934......	...	...	...	...	...	...	...	...
	1932......	...	...	...	...	...	...	...	...
	1930......	...	...	...	...	...	...	...	...
New Hampshire	1934......	17	113	10	123	425	843		1,268
	1932......	16	91	12	103	442	653		1,095
	1930.	14	87	6	93	493	491		984

TABLE I, *Continued*

States		No. Schools	Faculty			Students			
			Religious	Lay	Total	Boys	Girls	Unclassified	Total
New Jersey	1934	81	561	135	695	6,041	6,941		12,982
	1932	82	527	193	720	6,031	7,177	35	13,243
	1930	72	418	153	571	5,156	5,267	131	10,554
New Mexico	1934	8	43	4	47	321	544		865
	1932	10	56	12	68	399	745		1,144
	1930	11	48	6	54	384	498		882
New York	1934	223	1,632	332	1,964	17,578	22,513		40,091
	1932	224	1,713	484	2,197	19,032	22,246	88	41,366
	1930	206	1,493	453	1,930	16,203	19,435	192	35,830
North Carolina	1934	8	33	1	34	141	263		404
	1932	3	24	4	28	46	150		196
	1930	3	28	...	28	64	104		168
North Dakota	1934	14	84	3	87	369	587		956
	1932	15	96	6	102	395	603		998
	1930	15	76	1	77	254	509		763
Ohio	1934	145	1,011	174	1,185	9,626	11,314		20,940
	1932	146	1,004	179	1,183	10,123	12,557		22,680
	1930	151	976	195	1,171	9,382	12,566	116	22,064
Oklahoma	1934	32	55	9	64	624	734		1,358
	1932	23	100	9	109	561	709		1,270
	1930	31	112	11	123	582	852		1,434
Oregon	1934	19	119	16	135	519	1,242		1,761
	1932	20	111	16	149	649	1,242		1,891
	1930	22	131	13	144	596	992		1,588
Pennsylvania	1934	184	1,217	164	1,381	14,131	17,223		31,354
	1932	202	1,288	206	1,494	13,714	15,272	743	29,729
	1930	223	1,145	139	1,284	11,117	12,768	1,508	25,393
Rhode Island	1934	14	132	27	159	1,712	1,326		3,038
	1932	13	126	42	168	1,774	1,312		3,086
	1930	15	126	32	158	1,386	902	30	2,318
South Carolina	1934	2	17	3	20	161	228		389
	1932	4	21	1	22	130	220		350
	1930	4	19	...	19	115	193		308
South Dakota	1934	8	43	7	50	377	593		970
	1932	10	49	7	56	379	593	118	1,090
	1930	9	36	10	46	223	459		682
Tennessee	1934	12	69	13	82	760	820		1,580
	1932	8	69	11	80	489	475	714	1,678
	1930	9	62	13	75	446	383	714	1,543
Texas	1934	52	313	34	347	1,480	2,658		4,138
	1932	55	311	34	345	1,453	2,568		4,021
	1930	57	306	26	334	1,266	2,131	190	3,587
Utah	1934	5	35	5	40	108	188		296
	1932	4	27	9	36	101	267		368
	1930	4	21	3	24	98	270		368

TABLE I, *Continued*

States		No. Schools	Faculty			Students			
			Religious	Lay	Total	Boys	Girls	Unclassified	Total
Vermont	1934......	7	55	14	69	383	717		1,100
	1932......	9	57	16	73	383	842		1,225
	1930......	7	49	3	52	285	538		823
Virginia	1934......	22	93	6	99	683	871		1,554
	1932......	23	102	27	129	737	1,039		1,776
	1930......	20	83	7	90	447	967		1,414
Washington	1934......	22	201	10	211	1,053	1,207		2,260
	1932......	24	186	20	206	1,189	1,760		2,949
	1930......	27	168	24	192	1,182	1,600		2,782
West Virginia	1934......	15	47	5	52	519	671		1,190
	1932......	13	63	4	67	448	657		1,105
	1930......	13	70	1	71	366	637		1,003
Wisconsin	1934......	56	502	49	551	4,244	4,571		8,815
	1932......	50	437	61	498	3,209	4,112	82	7,403
	1930......	51	358	53	411	3,223	3,700	90	7,013
Wyoming	1934......	1	...	...	19	...	68		68
	1932......	1	4	...	12	...	32		44
	1930......	1	...	...	10	...	29		39

Religious, 11.7% lay teachers. Of the 13,258 Religious teachers, 2,828 or 21.4% were men and 10,430 or 78.6% were women. Students in 1934 numbered 271,786, of whom 118,305 or 43.5% were boys, and 153,481, or 56.5% were girls. In 1932 students numbered 273,339, with 3,045 unclassified as to sex; 43.1% were boys and 46.9 were girls. In 1934, students were 99.43% of the 1932 number—273,339—while 1932 showed an increase of 12.5% over the 1930 number of students, which totaled 241,925; 43% of these being boys and 57% girls.

Types of Secondary Schools and Names Assigned

Table II presents Catholic Secondary Schools for 1932 under the captions, "Type" and "Terminology," or names assigned. The types include Central, Parochial, Private or Independent, Institutional, and Juniorate. Central high schools (10.4%) admit students from an entire city in some cases, and in others, from many parishes; some are diocesan, that is, supported by funds from a diocese, as stated before, and some are multi-parochial, or supported by funds from co-operating parishes. The parochial high school (52.9%) supposedly admits only students from the one parish, but a review of original school re-

TABLE II

CATHOLIC SECONDARY SCHOOLS, 1932 SURVEY—TYPES AND TERMINOLOGY USED

	Parochial	Private	Central	Insti-tution	Junior-ate	High School	Acad-emy	Insti-tute	Prep. School	Junior High School	Comm. High School	Girls Semi-nary	Total
Total U. S.	1,096	737	215	10	15	1,236	602	32	18	56	120	9	2,073
%	52.9	35.6	10.4	.4	.7	59.6	29.04	1.55	.87	2.71	5.8	.43	100%
Alabama	9	7	2	..	1	12	6	1	..	..	..	..	19
Arizona	3	3	..	..	..	3	3	..	..	..	..	..	6
Arkansas	2	8	..	..	..	3	6	..	1	..	..	..	10
California	27	42	9	..	..	49	25	1	1	1	1	..	78
Colorado	10	6	..	..	..	11	4	..	..	1	..	..	16
Connecticut	3	8	1	..	..	3	7	..	..	..	2	..	12
Delaware	5	2	..	..	..	4	1	..	..	..	2	..	7
Dist. Columbia	8	8	..	..	..	5	9	..	..	..	1	1	16
Florida	6	11	..	..	..	8	9	..	..	..	..	..	17
Georgia	1	4	..	..	..	3	2	..	..	..	..	..	5
Idaho	2	4	..	..	..	1	5	..	..	..	..	..	6
Illinois	38	50	30	3	1	74	37	2	..	..	8	..	122
Indiana	22	15	10	..	..	25	14	..	..	4	4	..	47
Iowa	106	13	8	..	..	102	21	1	..	3	..	..	127
Kansas	25	10	8	..	1	34	8	..	..	2	..	..	44
Kentucky	20	25	8	..	2	29	22	..	..	1	3	..	55
Louisiana	27	32	..	..	..	38	19	1	..	..	1	..	59
Maine	2	5	4	..	..	7	2	..	..	..	2	..	11
Maryland	14	17	2	1	..	17	8	3	1	1	4	..	34
Massachusetts	82	22	7	..	..	76	21	..	1	6	7	..	111
Michigan	88	16	6	..	..	92	10	2	..	4	2	..	110
Minnesota	44	21	4	..	1	46	14	1	..	7	2	..	70
Mississippi	15	7	..	..	..	14	8	..	..	..	..	..	22
Missouri	26	24	5	..	..	28	23	1	..	2	1	..	55
Montana	2	6	3	..	..	7	4	..	..	..	..	..	11
Nebraska	38	10	..	..	..	32	11	..	..	3	2	..	48
*Nevada	..	..	..	..	..	..	..	..	..	..	..	..	..
New Hampshire	10	6	..	..	..	8	6	..	..	..	2	..	16
New Jersey	42	20	17	..	3	56	8	1	2	..	15	..	82
New Mexico	3	7	..	..	..	4	6	..	..	..	..	..	10
New York	92	107	23	1	1	73	103	13	2	9	20	4	224
No. Carolina	..	3	..	..	..	1	2	..	..	..	..	..	3
No. Dakota	2	12	1	..	..	7	8	..	..	..	..	..	15
Ohio	82	36	24	2	2	100	25	2	1	3	15	..	146
Oklahoma	14	8	1	..	..	15	8	..	..	..	..	..	23
Oregon	4	15	1	..	..	5	13	1	1	..	..	..	20
Pennsylvania	131	49	19	2	1	142	30	..	4	3	21	2	202
Rhode Island	4	4	5	..	..	3	8	..	..	1	..	1	13
So. Carolina	..	2	2	..	..	1	3	..	..	..	..	..	4
So. Dakota	8	2	..	..	..	7	3	..	..	..	..	..	10
Tennessee	2	5	1	..	..	5	3	..	..	..	..	..	8
Texas	12	38	5	..	..	16	36	..	1	1	1	..	55
Utah	2	2	..	..	..	1	2	..	..	1	..	..	4
Vermont	5	4	..	..	..	4	5	..	..	..	..	..	9
Virginia	15	7	..	1	..	11	9	2	..	..	1	..	23
Washington	7	15	2	..	..	12	12	..	..	..	..	..	24
West Virginia	8	3	2	..	..	9	4	..	..	1	..	..	13
Wisconsin	28	15	5	..	2	31	9	..	1	6	3	..	50
Wyoming	..	1	..	..	..	..	1	..	..	..	..	..	1

* Nevada has no Catholic secondary schools. Letter of Bishop, January 1935.

ports shows that a very great percentage of parochial high schools approximate central high schools, admitting students from other parishes upon payment of tuition either by the parish of the student, or by the student himself, while students of the supporting parish usually have free tuition. Parochial high schools have sometimes been named temporary central high schools, pending the erection of central high schools, and indicating both the need and the locality of the need.

TABLE III

CLASSIFICATION OF SCHOOLS FOR 1932 AND 1930

	1932				1930			
	Total Sec. Schools	Boys' Schools	Girls' Schools	Coed. Schools	Total Sec. Schools	Boys' Schools	Girls' Schools	Coed. Schools
Total U. S.......	2,073 100%	265 12.8%	695 33.53%	1,113 53.67%	2,124 100%	256 12.1%	715 33.6%	453 54.3%
Alabama........	19	4	5	10	14	3	5	6
Arizona.........	6	1	2	3	6	1	2	3
Arkansas........	10	2	2	6	10	2	2	6
California.......	78	17	48	13	78	14	48	16
Colorado........	16	2	4	10	17	2	4	11
Connecticut.....	12	1	10	1	10	1	8	1
Delaware........	7	1	3	3	8	1	3	4
Dist. of Columbia	16	2	10	4	16	2	10	4
Florida.........	17	3	4	10	16	3	4	9
Georgia.........	5	2	3	..	6	2	2	2
Idaho...........	6	1	2	3	7	1	1	5
Illinois..........	122	23	54	45	131	26	54	51
Indiana.........	47	6	20	21	47	4	19	24
Iowa...........	127	4	13	110	139	6	16	117
Kansas.........	44	2	11	31	45	3	11	31
Kentucky.......	55	5	18	32	67	4	23	40
Louisiana.......	59	13	26	20	60	15	28	17
Maine..........	11	3	6	2	11	3	6	2
Maryland.......	34	8	15	11	40	8	16	16
Massachusetts...	111	12	52	47	97	7	51	39
Michigan.......	110	8	16	86	119	8	16	95
Minnesota.......	70	9	19	42	66	8	13	45
Mississippi......	22	3	4	15	23	3	5	15
Missouri........	55	8	27	20	64	9	26	29
Montana........	11	2	4	5	12	3	5	4
Nebraska........	48	1	6	41	50	1	7	42
*Nevada........	..	..	..	..	..	..	..	..
New Hampshire.	16	3	9	4	14	4	8	2
New Jersey......	82	6	24	52	72	7	24	41
New Mexico....	10	1	2	7	11	1	4	6
New York......	224	37	90	97	206	34	91	81
North Carolina..	3	1	2	..	3	1	2	..

* Nevada has no Catholic secondary schools. Letter of Bishop, January 1935.

TABLE III, *Continued*

| | 1932 | | | | 1930 | | | |
	Total Sec. Schools	Boys' Schools	Girls' Schools	Coed. Schools	Total Sec. Schools	Boys' Schools	Girls' Schools	Coed. Schools
North Dakota...	15	1	1	13	15	1	2	12
Ohio...........	146	14	41	91	151	13	46	92
Oklahoma.......	23	3	5	15	31	3	7	21
Oregon.........	20	3	5	12	22	3	6	13
Pennsylvania....	202	18	58	126	223	18	58	147
Rhode Island....	13	6	5	2	15	6	7	2
South Carolina ..	4	..	3	1	4	..	3	1
South Dakota ...	10	..	1	9	9	..	1	8
Tennessee.......	8	2	4	2	9	2	4	3
Texas...........	55	11	22	22	57	10	24	23
Utah...........	4	..	1	3	4	..	2	2
Vermont........	9	..	3	6	7	..	3	4
Virginia........	23	5	6	12	20	2	8	10
Washington.....	24	6	14	4	27	6	15	6
West Virginia...	13	1	4	8	13	1	4	8
Wisconsin.......	50	4	12	34	51	4	11	36
Wyoming.......	1	..	..	1	1	..	..	1

Private or independent High Schools (35.6%) are those opened by Religious Communities at their own risk, in the absence of parochial and central high schools, or supplementing them, by request. Tuition is the ordinary means of support, and tuition costs range from $30.00 to $175.00 per year in most cases, though there are a few high-tuition schools. A review of the 1932 reports made the investigator wonder how the teachers were being supported in a great percentage of schools where only from one-tenth to one-half of the students paid full tuition, some of the others paying a small amount, and the rest nothing.

Some institutions, (0.4%) such as orphanages, industrial schools, and special schools for the blind, the deaf and other handicapped, present work on the secondary level as well as on the elementary.

Juniorates (0.7%) are high schools for the education of those who desire to enter the Religious Community which has the Juniorate. Admission to the initial step in such Religious Communities is not possible until secondary school work has been completed. Students are free to stay or to leave just as in the Novitiate of the Community.

As to terminology, it is noted that no name is indicative of the sex of the student except the Preparatory School, which name is used only for a boys' school. All other names are used for boys', girls' or co-educational schools. High Schools are 59.6%; academies, 29.04%; commer-

TABLE IV

BOY AND GIRL STUDENTS, URBAN AND RURAL, WITH TOTALS OF EACH

		Boys			Girls			Total		Grand Total	Unclassified
		Urban	Rural	Total	Urban	Rural	Total	Urban	Rural		
Total U. S.	1932	109,491	8,171	117,662	140,564	12,068	152,632	252,837	20,502	273,339	3,045
	1930			102,060			135,083	224,082	17,843	241,925	4,785
Alabama	1932	235	364	599	516	28	554	751	392	1,143	……
	1930			520			520	696	344	1,040	……
Arizona	1932	275	……	275	178	……	178	453	……	453	……
	1930			123			176	299	……	299	……
Arkansas	1932	177	70	247	405	……	405	582	70	652	……
	1930			222			364	526	60	586	……
*California	1932	4,440	172	4,612	6,432	306	6,738	10,872	553	11,425	75
	1930			3,676			6,159	9,667	428	10,095	……
Colorado	1932	950	4	954	1,034	53	1,087	1,984	57	2,041	……
	1930			823			1,034	1,779	78	1,857	……
Connecticut	1932	89	……	89	1,240	104	1,344	1,329	104	1,433	……
	1930			159			1,146	1,254	51	1,305	……
Delaware	1932	237	……	237	304	……	304	541	……	541	……
	1930			213			224	437	……	437	……
District of Columbia	1932	678	……	678	1,196	……	1,196	1,874	……	1,874	……
	1930			594			1,048	1,642	……	1,642	……
Florida	1932	376	76	452	757	177	934	1,133	253	1,386	……
	1930			428			683	888	223	1,111	……
Georgia	1932	338	……	338	324	……	324	662	……	662	……
	1930			396			233	629	……	629	……

* Indicates that there are unclassified students, so that the totals do not equal the sum of the figures.

TABLE IV, *Continued*

State	Year										
Idaho	1932	147	…	147	378	28	406	525	28	553	…
	1930	…	…	152	…	…	375	527	…	527	…
Illinois	1932	10,579	343	10,922	14,047	620	14,667	24,626	963	25,589	…
	1930	…	…	9,673	…	…	13,463	22,551	726	23,277	…
Indiana	1932	1,993	154	2,147	3,112	363	3,475	5,105	517	5,622	…
	1930	…	…	1,738	…	…	2,887	4,187	452	4,639	…
*Iowa	1932	2,501	1,497	3,998	3,374	1,840	5,214	6,020	3,407	9,427	215
	1930	…	…	3,286	…	…	4,845	5,308	2,823	8,131	…
Kansas	1932	1,167	320	1,487	1,627	451	2,078	2,794	771	3,565	…
	1930	…	…	1,517	…	…	2,027	2,507	1,037	3,544	…
Kentucky	1932	1,253	438	1,691	1,925	929	2,854	3,178	1,367	4,545	…
	1930	…	…	1,358	…	…	2,557	2,658	1,287	3,945	…
Louisiana	1932	2,549	103	2,652	2,498	262	2,760	5,047	365	5,412	…
	1930	…	…	2,160	…	…	2,514	4,369	305	4,674	…
Maryland	1932	1,740	331	2,071	1,295	461	1,756	3,035	792	3,827	…
	1930	…	…	1,931	…	…	1,780	2,937	858	3,795	…
Maine	1932	674	…	674	834	…	834	1,508	…	1,508	…
	1930	…	…	429	…	…	626	1,055	…	1,055	…
*Massachusetts	1932	5,567	…	5,567	9,315	176	9,491	15,786	176	15,962	904
	1930	…	…	5,185	…	…	8,220	14,227	104	14,331	…
*Michigan	1932	6,613	387	7,000	7,991	641	8,632	14,675	1,028	15,703	71
	1930	…	…	5,963	…	…	7,610	12,875	1,039	13,914	…
Minnesota	1932	2,695	745	3,440	3,173	885	4,058	5,868	1,630	7,498	…
	1930	…	…	3,119	…	…	3,618	5,246	1,509	6,755	…
Mississippi	1932	738	…	738	472	95	567	1,210	95	1,305	…
	1930	…	…	456	…	…	618	979	95	1,074	…

* Indicates that there are unclassified students, so that the totals do not equal the sum of the figures.

TABLE IV, *Continued*

		Boys			Girls			Total		Grand	
		Urban	Rural	Total	Urban	Rural	Total	Urban	Rural	Total	Unclassified
Missouri	1932	2,967	189	3,165	4,403	255	4,658	7,370	444	7,814	…
	1930	…	…	3,119	…	…	4,355	6,995	479	7,474	…
Montana	1932	455	…	466	920	…	920	1,386	…	1,386	…
	1930	…	…	520	…	…	828	1,348	…	1,348	…
Nebraska	1932	888	441	1,329	1,394	583	1,977	2,282	1,024	3,306	…
	1930	…	…	1,022	…	…	1,879	1,952	949	2,901	…
New Hampshire	1932	442	…	442	477	176	653	919	176	1,095	…
	1930	…	…	493	…	…	491	830	154	984	…
*New Jersey	1932	5,988	43	6,031	6,930	247	7,177	12,953	290	13,243	35
	1930	…	…	5,156	…	…	5,267	10,375	179	10,554	…
*New York	1932	18,811	221	19,032	21,420	826	22,246	40,319	1,047	41,366	88
	1930	…	…	16,203	…	…	19,435	35,090	740	35,830	…
North Carolina	1932	46	…	46	150	…	150	196	…	196	…
	1930	…	…	64	…	…	104	168	…	168	…
North Dakota	1932	157	238	395	333	270	603	490	508	998	…
	1930	…	…	254	…	…	509	428	335	763	…
Ohio	1932	9,819	304	10,123	11,968	589	12,447	12,787	893	22,680	…
	1930	…	…	9,382	…	…	12,569	21,336	728	22,064	…
Oklahoma	1932	544	17	561	661	48	709	1,205	65	1,270	…
	1930	…	…	582	…	…	852	1,285	149	1,434	…
Oregon	1932	495	154	649	1,011	231	1,242	1,506	385	1,891	…
	1930	…	…	596	…	…	992	1,295	293	1,588	…
*Pennsylvania	1932	13,453	261	13,714	14,995	277	15,272	29,191	538	29,729	743
	1930	…	…	11,117	…	…	12,768	24,885	508	25,393	…
Rhode Island	1932	1,774	…	1,774	1,312	…	1,312	3,086	…	3,086	…
	1930	…	…	1,386	…	…	902	2,318	…	2,318	…

* Indicates that there are unclassified students, so that the totals do not equal the sum of the figures.

TABLE IV, *Continued*

State	Year	Boys	Girls	Total	Boys	Girls	Total	Boys	Girls	Total	Uncl.
South Carolina	1932	130		130	220		220	350		350	
	1930			115			193	308		308	
*South Dakota	1932	249	130	379	370	223	593	619	471*	1,090	118
	1930			223			459	537	145	682	
*Tennessee	1932	489		489	475		475	1,678		1,678	714
	1930			446			383	1,543		1,543	
Texas	1932	1,280	173	1,453	2,331	237	2,568	3,611	410	4,021	
	1930			1,266			2,131	3,394	193	3,587	
Utah	1932	101		101	267		267	368		368	
	1930			98			270	368		368	
Vermont	1932	352	31	383	789	53	842	1,141	84	1,225	
	1930			285			538	712	111	823	
Virginia	1932	549	188	737	859	180	1,039	1,408	368	1,776	
	1930			447			967	1,260	154	1,414	
Washington	1932	1,004	185	1,189	1,579	181	1,760	2,583	366	2,949	
	1930			1,182			1,600	2,452	330	2,782	
West Virginia	1932	448		448	657		657	1,105		1,105	
	1930			366			637	1,003		1,003	
*Wisconsin	1932	2,622	587	3,209	3,848	264	4,112	6,552	851	7,403	82
	1930			3,223			3,700	6,098	915	7,013	
Wyoming	1932	12		12	32		32	44		44	
	1930	10		10			29	39		39	

* Indicates that there are unclassified students, so that the totals do not equal the sum of the figures.

cial high schools, 5.8%; junior high schools, 2.71%; Institutes, 1.55%; Preparatory Schools, 0.87%; and Girls' Seminary 0.43%.

Coeducational and Segregated Schools, 1932 and 1930

For comparative purposes, Table III presents boys', girls' and co-educational schools for 1932 and 1930. Percentages vary only a little, the greatest change being an increase of 0.7% in boys' schools.

Urban and Rural Totals

Table IV divides boys and girls according to urban and rural population, supplying totals for boys, girls, urban, and rural. In assigning students to urban and rural classification, use is made of the plan adopted by the United States of calling "rural" all those localities where the population is under 2,500 and "urban" all those localities where the population is over 2,500. This presents an anomaly in the metropolitan districts, and for small towns near large cities. Technically rural as to size of population, communication with large cities is so easy that the resources of these cities are available for educational and work opportunities. There can be found no plan which will adapt itself without some adjustment. The totals for rural students—7% of boys and 8% of girls or 7.5% of all—may be far from correct since bus and train transportation bring many into urban schools.

Comparison of Urban and Rural Schools and Students, Public and Catholic

Table V presents Catholic secondary schools and their enrollment according to population of the district, for 1932 and 1930, diffused to four sizes of cities, and to rural communities, retaining the connotation mentioned above. The division of urban localities was adopted from Bulletin 1931, No. 20, Office of Education, Department of the Interior, "Biennial Survey of Education in the United States, 1928-30, Statistics of Public High Schools, 1929-30." [82]

Comparative statistics for public secondary schools, 1930, are presented. Mention has already been made in Chapter I of the augmented totals in these, due to duplication in Negro schools, and the solution of the problem. The total of 22,237 public high schools reporting is 92.9% of the known total, as previously expressed. This division in

TABLE V

CATHOLIC SECONDARY SCHOOLS AND ENROLLMENT ACCORDING TO POPULATION, 1932 AND 1930, COMPARATIVE PUBLIC SCHOOL STATISTICS ACCORDING TO POPULATION, 1930

	Urban				Population of Cities								Rural	
					Over 100,000		30,000 to 99,999		10,000 to 29,999		2,500 to 9,999			
	Total Schools	Boys	Girls	Total Urban	Schools	No. of Pupils	Schools	No. of Pupils	Schools	No. of Pupils	Schools	No. of Pupils	Schools	No. of Pupils
Total	1,687	109,491	140,564	252,837	738	152,596	320	46,049	332	33,861	297	20,400	386	20,502
U.S. 1932	81.4%	40.56	51.42	92.5% of urban	35.6	55.46	15.5	16.84	16%	12.4	14.3	7.46	18.6	7.5 of all
Cath. H. S.	437% of rural H. S.				43.7	60.35	19%	18.2	19.7	13.39	17.6	8.06	22.88	8.1 of urban
Total	1,712			224,082	738	137,103	316	39,461	343	29,386	315	18,132	412	17,843
U.S. 1930	80.6% of all H.S.			92.6% of urban	34.74	56.66	14.87	16.311	16.14	12.147	14.83	7.494	19.4	7.375 of all
Cath. H. S.	415% of rural H. S.				43.1	61%	18.5	18%	20%	13%	18.5	8%	24%	8% of urban
Total Urban	5,484			3,701,363	1,062	1,623,064	682	602,857	1,116	665,805	2,624	809,637	16,736	1,455,544
U.S. 1930	24.68% of all H.S.			71.77% of all	4.78	31.47	3.07	11.7	5.03	12.91	11.81	15.7	75.32	28.23 of all
Public	32.7% of rural H.S.			254% of urban	19.36	43.9	12.4	16.2	20.3	18%	47.9	21.8	305%	39.3% of urban
Alabama '32	13	235	516	751	3	132	6	510	3	57	1	52	6	392
'30	11	...	...	696	3	159	5	420	2	65	1	52	3	344
Arizona '32	6	275	178	453	...	...	3	259	...	...	3	194	...	...
'30	6	...	...	299	...	...	3	202	...	...	3	97	...	...
Arkansas '32	9	177	406	582	...	...	4	393	2	88	3	101	1	70
'30	9	...	...	526	...	...	4	354	2	81	3	91	1	60
California '32	70	4,440	6,432	10,872	35	7,119	16	2,455	8	579	11	719	8	553*
'30	70	...	...	9,667	36	6,435	15	2,136	7	436	12	660	8	428

* Plus unclassified.

TABLE V, *Continued*

Population of Cities

State	Total Schools	Urban			Over 100,000		30,000 to 99,999		10,000 to 29,999		2,500 to 9,999		Rural	
		Boys	Girls	Total Urban	Schools	No. of Pupils	Schools	No. of Pupils	Schools	No. of Pupils	Schools	No. of Pupils	Schools	No. of Pupils
Colorado '32	14	950	1,034	1,984	5	889	2	536	3	220	4	339	2	57
'30	15	....	....	1,779	5	891	2	208	3	188	5	492	2	78
Connecticut '32	10	89	1,240	1,329	4	273	3	804	1	83	2	169	2	104
'30	9	....	....	1,254	2	263	3	592	2	271	2	128	1	51
Delaware '32	7	237	304	541	6	501					1	40		
'30	8	....	....	437	7	412					1	25		
Dist. of Columbia '32	16	678	1,196	1,874	16	1,874								
'30	16	....	....	1,642	16	1,642								
Florida '32	12	376	757	1,133	4	462	1	51	4	437	3	183	5	253
'30	12	....	....	888	4	429	1	42	5	381	2	36	4	223
Georgia '32	5	338	324	662	2	320	3	342						
'30	6	....	....	629	2	301	4	328						
Idaho '32	5	147	378	525					2	321	3	204	1	28
'30	7	....	....	527					3	329	4	198		
Illinois '32	101	10,579	14,047	24,626	45	16,137	26	5,330	16	1,734	14	1,416	21	963
'30	110	....	....	22,551	56	15,352	23	4,355	16	1,561	15	1,283	21	726
Indiana '32	40	1,993	3,112	5,105	17	3,406	6	680	11	625	6	394	7	517
'30	37	....	....	4,137	12	2,426	7	642	11	635	7	384	10	452
Iowa '32	57	2,501	3,374	*6,020	2	386	22	2,917	18	1,636	15	1,081	70	3,407
'30	63	....	....	5,308	2	393	22	2,419	19	1,601	20	895	76	2,823
Kansas '32	21	1,167	1,627	2,794	4	958	1	276	9	990	7	570	23	771
'30	22	....	....	2,507	4	738	1	242	9	984	8	543	23	1,037
Kentucky '32	28	1,253	1,925	3,178	10	1,746	6	690	7	589	5	153	27	1,367
'30	33	....	....	2,658	10	1,343	7	588	9	541	7	186	34	1,287

* Plus unclassified.

TABLE V, Continued

Louisiana '32	49	2,549	2,498	5,047	19	3,279	4	371	9	559	17	838	10	365
'30	49	...	...	4,369	18	2,536	4	407	9	609	18	827	11	305
Maine '32	11	674	834	1,508	...	...	3	541	4	640	4	327	...	...
'30	11	...	...	1,055	...	...	3	461	4	395	4	199	...	...
Maryland '32	23	1,740	1,295	3,035	14	2,292	4	482	2	103	3	158	11	792
'30	28	...	...	2,937	18	2,380	4	320	2	75	4	162	12	858
Massachusetts '32	108	5,567	9,315	15,786*	51	9,532	36	4,090	19	2,044	2	120	3	176
'30	95	...	...	14,227	45	8,472	31	4,202	17	1,449	2	104	2	104
Michigan '32	86	6,613	7,991	14,675*	41	8,096	21	3,365	14	2,277	10	937	24	1,028
'30	93	...	...	12,875	43	7,265	22	2,793	17	2,070	11	747	26	1,039
Minnesota '32	38	2,695	3,173	5,868	19	3,701	...	...	9	1,287	10	880	32	1,630
'30	35	...	...	5,246	16	3,525	...	...	9	1,167	10	554	31	1,509
Mississippi '32	21	738	472	1,210	...	...	4	166	8	552	9	492	1	95
'30	22	...	...	979	...	...	3	110	11	523	8	346	1	95
Missouri '32	45	2,967	4,403	7,370	23	5,598	6	512	7	532	10	728	10	444
'30	50	...	...	6,995	23	5,321	6	587	6	375	15	712	14	479
Montana '32	11	466	920	1,386	...	...	2	636	6	557	3	193	...	...
'30	12	...	...	1,348	...	...	2	540	7	607	3	201	...	...
Nebraska '32	27	888	1,394	2,282	11	1,169	1	297	5	176	10	640	21	1,024
'30	27	...	...	1,952	11	1,088	1	123	5	211	10	530	23	949
New Hampshire '32	13	442	477	919	...	...	8	582	5	337	...	...	3	176
'30	11	...	...	830	...	...	8	668	3	162	...	...	3	154
New Jersey '32	80	5,988	6,930	12,953*	33	6,378	18	3,251	17	2,270	12	1,054	2	290
'30	70	...	...	10,375	29	5,448	17	2,347	15	1,727	9	853	2	179

* Plus unclassified.

TABLE V, Continued

| | | Urban | | | | Population of Cities | | | | | | | | Rural | |
| | | | | | | Over 100,000 | | 30,000 to 99,999 | | 10,000 to 29,999 | | 2,500 to 9,999 | | | |
State		Total Schools	Boys	Girls	Total Urban	Schools	No. of Pupils	Schools	No. of Pupils	Schools	No. of Pupils	Schools	No. of Pupils	Schools	No. of Pupils
New York	'32	208	18,811	21,420	40,319*	139	31,650	27	4,045	27	3,670	15	954	16	1,047
	'30	191	....	....	35,090	125	28,068	23	3,190	29	2,972	14	860	15	740
New Mexico	'32	9	394	736	1,130	....	....	....	....	4	651	5	479	1	14
	'30	9	....	....	820	....	....	....	....	4	476	5	344	2	62
North Carolina	'32	3	46	150	196	1	73	....	....	....	....	2	123	....	....
	'30	3	....	....	168	1	77	....	....	....	....	2	91	....	....
North Dakota	'32	6	157	333	490	....	....	....	....	2	245	4	245	9	508
	'30	6	....	....	428	....	....	....	....	2	187	4	241	9	335
Ohio	'32	129	9,819	11,968	21,787	69	14,898	20	3,589	17	1,780	23	1,520	17	893
	'30	134	....	....	21,336	71	15,145	24	3,003	16	1,751	23	1,437	17	728
Oklahoma	'32	21	544	661	1,205	5	529	1	72	7	319	8	285	2	65
	'30	25	....	....	1,285	6	529	2	80	8	400	9	276	6	149
Oregon	'32	16	495	1,011	1,506	6	992	....	....	5	267	5	317	4	385
	'30	17	....	....	1,295	6	771	....	....	5	267	6	257	5	293
Pennsylvania	'32	192	13,453	14,995	29,191*	87	18,587	22	3,828	40	4,091	43	2,685	10	538
	'30	207	....	....	24,885	95	15,488	24	3,451	41	3,349	47	2,617	16	508
Rhode Island	'32	13	1,774	1,312	3,086	4	1,859	4	561	4	591	1	75	....	....
	'30	15	....	....	2,318	4	1,206	5	521	5	514	1	77	....	....
South Carolina	'32	4	130	220	350	....	....	3	336	....	....	1	14	....	....
	'30	4	....	....	308	....	....	3	294	....	....	1	14	....	....
South Dakota	'32	4	249	370	619	....	....	1	215	2	343	1	61	6	471*
	'30	5	....	....	537	....	....	1	215	2	243	1	79	4	145
Tennessee	'32	8	489	475	1,678*	8	1,678	....	....	....	....	....	....	....	....
	'30	9	....	....	1,543	9	1,543	....	....	....	....	....	....	....	....

* Plus unclassified.

TABLE V, *Concluded*

Texas	.32	48	1,280	2,331	3,611	21	2,063	12	867	10	501	5	180	7	410
	.30	50	...	...	2,394	22	2,029	11	714	11	461	6	190	7	193
Utah	.32	4	101	267	368	2	181	2	187	...	...	...	...	...	...
	.30	4	...	...	368	2	270	2	98	...	...	...	...	...	...
Vermont	.32	7	352	789	1,141	...	...	...	...	3	746	4	395	2	84
	.30	5	...	...	712	...	...	...	...	3	647	2	65	2	111
Virginia	.32	19	549	859	1,408	10	832	5	355	3	196	1	25	4	368
	.30	18	...	...	1,260	10	844	5	272	2	127	1	17	2	154
Washington	.32	18	1,004	1,579	2,583	14	2,242	2	92	4	341	...	...	6	366
	.30	21	...	...	2,452	15	2,006	6	682	4	354	...	...	6	330
West Virginia	.32	13	448	657	1,105	...	...	6	609	5	321	2	102	...	...
	.30	13	...	...	1,003	...	...	6	...	5	264	2	130	...	...
Wisconsin	.32	38	2,622	3,848	6,552*	9	2,837	11	1,695	9	1,062	9	958	12	851
	.30	38	...	...	6,098	9	2,395	10	1,779	9	892	10	1,032	13	915
Wyoming	.32	1	12	32	44	...	...	...	...	1	44	...	...	...	...
	.30	1	10	29	39	...	...	...	...	1	39	...	...	...	...

* Plus unclassified.

Table V into urban and rural districts accounts for 22,220 schools, resulting in an error of 17 schools.

An examination of the data in Table V reveals a striking contrast between public and Catholic high schools. In 1930, public urban high schools were 24.68%, that is, one-fourth of total public high schools and 32.7%, one-third of rural public high schools; Catholic urban high schools formed 80.6%, that is, four-fifths of all Catholic high schools, and 415%, more than four times the number of Catholic rural high schools. As to students, public urban high schools, less than one-fourth of the total public high schools, cared for 71.77% of all public high school students, Catholic urban high schools or 80.8% of all, instructed 92.6% of all Catholic high school students. The average number of students in public urban high schools, 1930 was 676.17; in Catholic urban high schools, 130.88. (The 1932 average was 150.)

Public rural high schools, 75.32% of total public high schools, enroll 28.23% of the total public high school students, and 39.3% of the urban, with an average of 87 students. Catholic rural high schools form only 19.4% of all Catholic high schools, and 24% of Catholic urban high schools, and enroll 7.37% of all Catholic high school students, 8% of urban Catholic high school students; they show an average of 43.3 students. When we examine further we note even more the concentration of Catholic high schools and students in 88 cities with populations over 100,000. In this class of cities are 34.74% of all Catholic high schools, and 43.1% of urban Catholic high schools, with 56.66% of all Catholic students, and 61% of all urban Catholic students. In this size of city, public high schools are 4.78% of all public high schools, with 31.47% of all public high school students. This connotes very large public high schools in the largest cities.

In the second class of cities, of population 30,000 to 99,999, Catholic high schools are 14.87% of all Catholic high schools, with 16.31% of all Catholic high school students; public high schools in this same class of cities are 3.07% of all public high schools, with 11.7% of all public high school students. In cities of population 10,000 to 29,999, Catholic high schools are 16.14% of all Catholic high schools, with 12.15% of all Catholic high school students; public high schools form 5.03% of all public high schools with 12.91% of all public high school students. Cities with population 2,500 to 9,999 have 14.83% of Catholic high schools with 7.49% of all Catholic high school students; of public high schools these cities have 11.81% of all public high schools with 15.7% of all public high school students.

The 1932 census showed a relatively small decrease in Catholic high schools due in some cases to consolidation, in others to closing of schools, but this decrease was principally in rural Catholic high schools. School census, however, in rural Catholic high schools increased, so that the average number of students was 53.1, yet the rate of increase for rural Catholic high schools was slightly lower than for urban Catholic high schools (1.13% and 1.15% respectively).

Sizes of High Schools and Numbers of Each Type

Table VI answers questions relative to range of sizes of Catholic high schools, number and percentage of each, and comparative data for public high schools. Catholic high school statistics are given for 1932 and 1930, public high schools for 1930. In some classifications, adjustment was necessary because division of public and Catholic high school size was not made on the same basis. Paralleling the custom of federal reports, high schools with fewer than 10 students are not counted, since such a small group is a courtesy to patrons, rather than an organized school. Public high school figures are taken from Bulletin 1931, No. 20, Office of Education, Department of the Interior.

For 1930, Catholic high schools with fewer than 25 students were 13.5% of all Catholic high schools; public high schools had 9.34% of this size. In the next group having from 25 to 49 students, Catholic high schools had 22.5% while public high schools had 17.38%. In both Catholic and public high schools, the mode is found in the third group having from 50 to 99 students; in Catholic schools the percentage was 29.5, while public high schools had 27.26%. Catholic high schools with students ranging from 100 to 199 formed 21.2% of the total, while public high schools in this classification formed 20.7%. In the next higher group with students from 200 to 299, percentages take a sharp drop, Catholic high schools showing 6.1% and public high schools, 8.34%. High schools having from 300 to 500 students formed 4.4% of Catholic schools and 6.44% of public schools. High schools having from 500 to 1,000 students formed 2.4% of all Catholic high schools and 6.34% of public high schools. High schools with

TABLE VI

Size of Catholic High Schools, 1932 and 1930; Comparative Figures for Public High Schools, 1930

	Total High Schools	Under 25	25–49	50–74	75–99	100–199	200–299	300–399	400–499	500–599	600–699	700–799	800–899	900–999	1,000–1,249	1,250–1,499	1,500–1,999	2,000–2,499	2,500–3,000	Negro High Schools Unreported
Total U. S. 1932	2,073	212	401	336	245	527	175	75	31	24	13	9	8	7	3	1	1	3	1	21
Catholic H. S. 100%		10.23	19.34	16.2	11.82	25.4	8.44	3.61	1.5	1.2	.62	.43	.4	.33	.14	.05	.10	.14	.05	..
Total U. S. 1930	2,124	286	479	627		448	129	95			50				10					22
Catholic H. S. 100%		13.5	22.5	29.5		21.2	6.1	4.4			2.4				.5					..
Total U. S. 1930	22,220	2,077	3,521 2,543	3,866		4,603	1,633	1,478			1,421				934			161, up to 10,000 Students		
Public H. S. 100%		9.34	17.38	15.83 11.43 27.26		20.7	8.34	6.44			6.34				4.2					.72
Alabama '32	19	6	4	4	1	4														2
'30	14	3	2	5	4	..														2
Arizona '32	6	..	2	1	1	2														
'30	6	1	3	1	1	1														
Arkansas '32	10	1	4	2	..	3														2
'30	10	1	4	3		2														2
California '32	78	5	5	17	8	27	7	3	4	1	1									
'30	78	7	11	21		27	5	2	3		1									
Colorado '32	16	1	3	3	1	6	..	2												
'30	17	1	2	6		5	2	1												

Figures, 1932—from original school reports; 1930, Catholic High Schools from Directory, Catholic Schools and Colleges, 1931–33; Public High School figures from U. S. Office of Education, Department of Interior, Bulletin, 1931, No. 20. Biennial Survey of Education in United States. Page 1 shows 22,137 high schools; Tables 36–19 inclusive, showed duplication in Negro schools. Corrected by Office of Education so that there is here an error of 17, that is, 22,120 public high schools. Complete correction was not possible.

TABLE VI, Continued

State	Year													
Connecticut	'32	12	1	1	3	4	2	:	:	1	:	:	:	1
	'30	10	:	2	3	3	3	1	:	:	:	:	:	:
Delaware	'32	7	1	4	:	3	1	1	:	:	:	:	:	1
	'30	8	2	4	:	2	1	1	:	:	:	:	:	:
District of Columbia	'32	16	1	2	2	3	3	2	:	:	:	:	:	:
	'30	16	:	4	8	2	2	1	:	1	:	:	:	:
Florida	'32	17	2	4	4	4	4	1	:	:	:	:	2	2
	'30	16	2	5	6	3	3	1	:	:	:	:	1	2
Georgia	'32	5	:	:	1	4	4	:	:	:	:	:	:	:
	'30	6	:	:	2	:	4	:	:	:	:	:	:	:
Idaho	'32	6	:	2	1	1	1	:	:	:	:	:	:	:
	'30	7	:	4	2	2	1	:	1	:	:	:	:	:
Illinois	'32	122	6	19	14	23	20	4	8	5	4	1	2	2
	'30	131	8	24	34	29	10	11	4	5	1	2	1	2
Indiana	'32	47	5	10	7	9	5	2	:	1	:	:	:	:
	'30	47	7	10	15	10	4	:	:	1	:	:	:	:
Iowa	'32	127	20	31	27	29	2	2	1	:	:	:	:	1
	'30	139	32	45	42	17	2	1	:	:	:	:	:	1
Kansas	'32	44	10	10	10	5	3	1	:	:	:	:	:	:
	'30	45	9	11	14	5	5	:	:	:	:	:	:	1
Kentucky	'32	55	9	13	14	10	1	:	:	1	:	:	:	1
	'30	67	21	14	21	10	:	:	:	:	:	:	:	1

Figures, 1932—from original school reports; 1930, Catholic High Schools from Directory, Catholic Schools and Colleges, 1932–33. Public High School figures from U. S. Office of Education, Department of Interior, Bulletin, 1931, No. 20. Biennial Survey of Education in United States. Page 1 shows 22,237 high schools; Tables 36–39 inclusive, showed duplication in Negro schools. Corrected by Office of Education so that there is here an error of 17, that is, 22,120 public high schools. Complete correction was not possible.

TABLE VI, *Continued*

States		Total High Schools	Under 25	25–49	50–74	75–99	100–199	200–299	300–399	400–499	500–599	600–699	700–799	800–899	900–999	1,000–1,249	1,250–1,499	1,500–1,999	2,000–2,499	2,500–3,000	Negro High Schools Unreported
Louisiana	'32	59	4	19	13	9	9	1	2	1		1										6
	'30	60	7	20	21	9	7	3	1													6
Maine	'32	11	1	1	1	2	3	2	1													
	'30	11	2	1	4	3	1															
Maryland	'32	34	6	4	8	4	6	3	2	1												
	'30	40	9	6	13		8		3	1												
Massachusetts	'32	111	8	21	11	10	37	16	5		1					1	1					
	'30	97	7	15	27		28	11	5		1				1	1	1					
Michigan	'32	110	7	14	12	13	35	19	8	2												
	'30	119	10	23	21	10	31	20	2	2												
Minnesota	'32	70	8	22	7	10	16	2	2	1												
	'30	66	10	17	21		10	2	3	1				1								
Mississippi	'32	22	5	9	4	2		2														1
	'30	23	9	6	7																	1
Missouri	'32	55	5	9	10	5	9	12	2		1			1	1							
	'30	64	9	18	13		14	4	3	1				2								
Montana	'32	11		1	2	1	4	1	2													
	'30	12	2	2	7	1	1															
Nebraska	'32	48	10	15	6	9	5	2	1													
	'30	50	14	11	18		6		1													
New Hampshire	'32	16	5	2	3	2	3	1														
	'30	14	1	6	4		3															

Figures, 1932—from original school reports; 1930, Catholic High Schools from Directory, Catholic Schools and Colleges, 1932–33. Public High School figures from U. S. Office of Education, Department of Interior, Bulletin, 1931, No. 20. Biennial Survey of Education in United States, Page 1 shows 22,237 high schools; Tables 36–39 inclusive, showed duplication in Negro schools. Corrected by Office of Education so that there is here an error of 17, that is, 22,220 public high schools. Complete correction was not possible.

TABLE VI, Continued

State	Year																					
New Jersey	'32	82	6	17	12	7	18	8	7	1	3	2	:	:	:	:	:	1	:	:	:	:	:
	'30	72	8	14	20	:	16	3	5	2	:	2	2	:	:	:	:	:	:	:	:	1	1
New Mexico	'32	10	1	:	:	2	6	1	:	:	:	:	:	:	:	:	:	:	:	:	:	:	:
	'30	11	2	2	2	:	5	:	:	:	:	:	:	:	:	:	:	:	:	:	:	:	:
New York	'32	224	16	27	25	28	73	20	14	7	4	2	2	:	:	1	2	1	1	:	:	1	1
	'30	206	15	33	50	:	61	16	16	2	3	1	1	1	2	2	1	2	1	:	:	1	1
North Carolina	'32	3	:	1	1	:	:	:	:	:	:	:	:	:	:	:	:	:	:	:	:	:	:
	'30	3	:	1	2	1	:	:	:	:	:	:	:	:	:	:	:	:	:	:	:	:	:
North Dakota	'32	15	2	3	6	:	4	:	:	:	:	:	:	:	:	:	:	:	:	:	:	:	:
	'30	15	3	5	6	:	1	:	:	:	:	:	:	:	:	:	:	:	:	:	:	:	:
Ohio	'32	146	13	26	23	15	34	15	8	2	4	2	1	1	:	:	1	:	1	:	:	1	1
	'30	151	13	31	34	:	43	13	6	5	2	1	1	:	:	:	:	:	:	:	:	1	1
Oklahoma	'32	23	4	9	7	:	3	:	:	:	:	:	:	:	:	:	:	:	:	:	:	:	:
	'30	31	7	11	12	:	1	:	:	:	:	:	:	:	:	:	:	:	:	:	:	:	:
Oregon	'32	20	2	3	5	2	6	1	1	:	:	:	:	:	:	:	:	:	:	:	:	:	:
	'30	22	3	8	6	:	3	2	:	:	:	:	:	:	:	:	:	:	:	:	:	:	:
Pennsylvania	'32	202	23	41	26	31	58	11	2	2	2	2	:	1	:	:	1	:	1	2	1	1	1
	'30	223	35	53	78	37	9	9	2	1	2	:	1	:	1	:	:	1	:	3	1	:	:
Rhode Island	'32	13	:	:	:	:	9	:	:	1	:	:	1	:	1	:	:	:	:	:	:	:	:
	'30	15	:	4	3	2	6	:	:	:	:	:	:	:	:	:	:	:	:	:	:	:	:
South Carolina	'32	4	2	1	:	:	1	1	:	:	:	:	:	:	:	:	:	:	:	:	:	:	:
	'30	4	2	1	:	:	1	1	:	:	:	:	:	:	:	:	:	:	:	:	:	:	:

Figures, 1931—from original school reports; 1930, Catholic High Schools from Directory, Catholic Schools and Colleges, 1932-33. Public High School figures from U. S. Office of Education, Department of Interior, Bulletin, 1931, No. 20. Biennial Survey of Education in United States. Page 1 shows 22,237 high schools; Tables 36-39 inclusive, showed duplication in Negro schools. Corrected by Office of Education so that there is here an error of 17, that is, 22,220 public high schools. Complete correction was not possible.

TABLE VI, *Concluded*

States	Total High Schools	Under 25	25-49	50-74	75-99	100-199	200-299	300-399	400-499	500-599	600-699	700-799	800-899	900-999	1,000-1,249	1,250-1,499	1,500-1,999	2,000-2,499	2,500-3,000	Negro High Schools Unreported
South Dakota '32	10	1	1	2	1	3	2	…	…	…	…	…	…	…	…	…	…	…	…	…
'30	9	1	2	…	…	…	1	…	…	…	…	…	…	…	…	…	…	…	…	…
Tennessee '32	8	…	…	2	…	4	1	…	…	…	…	1	…	…	…	…	…	…	…	1
'30	9	…	…	5	…	2	1	…	…	…	…	1	…	…	…	…	…	…	…	1
Texas '32	55	4	16	16	3	15	1	…	…	…	…	…	…	…	…	…	…	…	…	2
'30	57	12	18	15	…	11	1	…	…	…	…	…	…	…	…	…	…	…	…	2
Utah '32	4	1	…	1	…	2	…	…	…	…	…	…	…	…	…	…	…	…	…	…
'30	4	1	…	1	…	2	…	…	…	…	…	…	…	…	…	…	…	…	…	…
Vermont '32	9	1	…	3	…	3	1	1	…	…	…	…	…	…	…	…	…	…	…	…
'30	7	1	2	1	…	2	…	1	…	…	…	…	…	…	…	…	…	…	…	…
Virginia '32	23	1	7	5	1	9	…	…	…	…	…	…	…	…	…	…	…	…	…	…
'30	20	2	4	10	…	4	…	…	…	…	…	…	…	…	…	…	…	…	…	…
Washington '32	24	2	3	5	2	8	2	2	…	…	…	…	…	…	…	…	…	…	…	…
'30	27	3	7	5	…	7	5	…	…	…	…	…	…	…	…	…	…	…	…	…
West Virginia '32	13	…	1	6	4	2	…	…	…	…	…	…	…	…	…	…	…	…	…	…
'30	13	…	1	9	…	2	…	…	…	…	…	…	…	…	…	…	…	…	…	…
Wisconsin '32	50	5	11	4	6	12	6	2	2	1	1	…	…	…	…	…	…	…	…	…
'30	51	5	11	13	6	9	4	6	1	2	…	…	…	…	…	…	…	…	…	…
Wyoming '32	1	…	1	…	…	…	…	…	…	…	…	…	…	…	…	…	…	…	…	…
'30	1	…	1	…	…	…	…	…	…	…	…	…	…	…	…	…	…	…	…	…

Figures, 1932—from original school reports; 1930, Catholic High Schools from Directory, Catholic Schools and Colleges, 1932–33; Public High School figures from U. S. Office of Education, Department of Interior, Bulletin, 1931, No. 20. Biennial Survey of Education in United States. Page 1 shows 22,237 high schools; Tables 36–39 inclusive, showed duplication in Negro schools. Corrected by Office of Education so that there is here an error of 17, that is, 22,220 public high schools. Complete correction was not possible.

TABLE VII

ACCREDITATION OF CATHOLIC SECONDARY SCHOOLS, 1932

Accrediting Agencies: State Department of Education; State Universities: Regional; Middle States, North Central, Southern Association, Northwestern Association; National Catholic Education Association; Catholic University of America.

	Total H. S.	Total Accredited	Per Cent Accredited	Accredited to More Than One
Total U. S. 1932...............	2,073	1,496	72.1	386—18.6%
Alabama.....................	19	10	52.6	1
Arizona.....................	6	6	100	1
Arkansas....................	10	9	90	3
California...................	78	60	77	8
Colorado....................	16	16	100	5
Connecticut.................	12	10	83.3	6
Delaware....................	7	3	43	1
District of Columbia..........	16	13	81.25	1
Florida.....................	17	11	65	2
Georgia.....................	5	5	100	1
Idaho......................	6	6	100	2
Illinois.....................	122	102	83.6	73
Indiana.....................	47	34	72.34	8
Iowa.......................	127	96	75.6	18
Kansas.....................	44	41	93.18	12
Kentucky...................	55	40	72.72	14
Louisiana...................	59	56	95	8
Maine......................	11	9	81.8	..
Maryland...................	34	26	76.5	8
Massachusetts...............	111	27	24.32	7
Michigan...................	110	84	76.36	27
Minnesota..................	70	38	54.3	12
Mississippi.................	22	14	63.63	3
Missouri....................	55	49	89.09	22
Montana...................	11	10	90.9	3
Nebraska...................	48	34	70.83	5
*Nevada	..	..	..	..
New Hampshire..............	16	9	56.2	4
New Jersey..................	82	52	63.4	10
New Mexico.................	10	10	100	1
New York...................	224	181	80.8	18
North Carolina..............	3	3	100	1
North Dakota...............	15	8	53.3	1
Ohio.......................	146	104	71.23	21
Oklahoma...................	23	18	78.3	..
Oregon.....................	20	17	85	4
Pennsylvania................	202	134	66.33	31
Rhode Island................	13	10	77.7	3
South Carolina..............	4	3	75	..
South Dakota...............	10	7	70	2
Tennessee...................	8	5	62.5	3

TABLE VII, *Continued*

	Total H. S.	Total Accredited	Per Cent Accredited	Accredited to More Than One
Texas......................	55	41	74.5	6
Utah.......................	4	2	50	..
Vermont....................	9	6	66.6	3
Virginia...................	23	16	70	2
Washington.................	24	17	70.8	10
West Virginia..............	13	9	69.23	1
Wisconsin..................	50	34	68	14
Wyoming...................	1	1	100	..

* Nevada has no Catholic secondary schools. Letter of Bishop, January 1935.

students ranging from 1,000 to 2,000 formed 0.5% of Catholic schools, and 4.2% of public schools. While Catholic high schools ended with the last classification, public high schools ranged on up to 10,000 students, statistics showing that there were 161 or 0.72% from 2,000 up to and including 10,000 students: 38.3% of all public high school students were enrolled in high schools having more than 1,000 pupils.

Standards of High Schools

The accreditation of Catholic secondary schools for 1932 is presented in Table VII. These figures were secured from the original school reports and checked with Bulletin 1934, No. 17, Office of Education, Department of the Interior, "Accredited Secondary Schools in the United States." [83] A 1935 dissertation on *Effects of Accreditation on Catholic Secondary Schools* by Rev. J. T. O'Dowd, [84] states that in 1934, 66% of all Catholic high schools were accredited to State Departments of Education and State Universities, together with the four accrediting agencies, North Central, Middle States, Southern Association and Northwestern. The present investigation recognizes also accreditation to the National Catholic Education Association, and to the Catholic University of America, whose pioneer efforts in the accrediting of Catholic secondary schools deserves mention and commendation. Table VII shows 72.1% accredited, and of these, 18.6% were accredited to more than one Agency.

Summary

We have had a cursory view of the inception of Catholic secondary education, first mentioned in Florida in 1608, through the period of the Jesuit classical Manor Schools for boys in Maryland, begun during the first half of the seventeenth century, and extended to New York in 1682; we have noticed the beginning of a secondary school for girls; we have seen in 1802 the practical or vocational subjects added to the high school curriculum in the comprehensive plans of the Michigan schools; we have noted the legislation regarding education in the Provincial Councils of Cincinnati, [76] and the Plenary Councils of Baltimore, particularly the Third Plenary Council [77] which devoted one-fourth of its decrees to educational legislation. We have seen that secondary education was associated for a long time with higher education in the college preparatory departments, but later separated mainly through the establishment of parish secondary schools. We noticed the fact that when the Committee on High Schools of the National Catholic Education Association made its first report in 1910 there were approximately 400 high schools, exclusive of college preparatory departments; that the first survey conducted of Catholic secondary schools was made in 1915; that by the establishment of the Department of Education of the National Catholic Welfare Conference, regular biennial surveys were assured.

Catholic secondary schools now are found in the District of Columbia and in every state except Nevada. From 1930 to 1932 there was a decrease of 2% in number of schools, but 1932-34 showed an increase of 4%. Decrease may have been due to consolidation of schools, to the closing of schools because of financial stress, or to a "more intelligent high school building program." From 1915 to 1934 the number of schools was increased 70%.

Figure 2 pictures the rapid increase in schools and also in faculty, from 1915 to 1934. Table I shows that there was a decrease in faculty, in 1932-34, to the extent of 6.3%, 2% decrease in Religious Teachers, the remainder in Lay Teachers. The total increase in faculty, from 1915 to 1934 as pictured in Figure 2 was 579%. Students increased in number 12.5% from 1930-32. For the first time, the number of students in Catholic secondary schools decreased by one-half of one per cent from 1932 to 1934, according to the writer's statistics. However, the rapid growth in students from 75,000 to 271,786 during the period 1915 to 1934 was an increase of 364.4%.

Table III shows a comparison of 1932 and 1930 statistics for boys', girls', and coeducational high schools. Coeducational schools have decreased slightly in number; girls' schools have shown an increase, although girls seemed to have been more amply provided for in the past years than boys; boys' schools show a slight increase in number. Dr. Francis Crowley stated that boys were 42% of the Catholic high school population and girls 58% in 1926; in public high schools in the same year, boys formed 48% and girls 52%. By 1932 boys were 43.5% and girls 56.5% of the school population in Catholic secondary school; in public high schools boys were 49.2% and girls 50.8%. [83]

It is interesting to note in relation to early prejudices against the education of girls, that in 1932 there were almost three times as many Catholic high schools for girls as there were for boys, and that girl students in Catholic high schools exceeded boys by almost 30%.

Table II shows seven titles were used in referring to Catholic secondary schools. The name Preparatory school was indicative of a boys' school. All other titles were used for all three classifications of schools, boys', girls', and coeducational.

Five types are shown in Table II—parochial 1,096 or 52.9% in 1932; private schools in number 737 or 35.6%; central high schools 215 or 10.4%; 10 institutional high schools, 0.4% (orphanages, blind, deaf); and 15 juniorates or 0.7%. Of these schools, 56 were arranged on the 6-3-3 plan of junior-senior high schools, 35 were 3-year junior high schools; 117 were 2-year junior high schools and 1,865 were four-year high schools. From the individual school reports and from questionnaires in this investigation, it is apparent that many schools in the junior high school groups have developed or are in the process of developing into four-year high schools. The trend in types of schools is toward the central high school. Dr. Crowley showed that these central high schools in 1922 cared for 5.5% of students. [85] Dr. Carl J. Ryan showed in 1926 that 17.6% of all students in Catholic secondary schools were in 35 central high schools. [61] Dr. Crowley indicated that the number of central high schools had increased to 87 in 1930; 1932 reports used in Table II of the present investigation show 215 central high schools, which have 26.6% of all students, an increase of 9% in the six years from 1926 to 1932.

Table VI presents figures relative to sizes of high schools arranged in 18 groups for 1932 and 1930, with comparative figures for public high schools, 1930. In the 1932 census, 10.23% of Catholic high schools had an enrollment of fewer than 25 students, 19.34% had students numbering from 25 to 49; in other words, 29.57% of Catholic high schools had fewer than 50 students. Dr. Crowley stated that one-third of the schools in 1926 had an enrollment of fewer than 50 students. [85] Since the exact percentage was not stated in his article, comparison cannot be made, but the writer believes—from a close study—that there has been a reduction in the percentage of these small schools from 1926 to 1930. This is clearly indicated by a comparison of 1930 and 1932 percentages, 36% and 29.57% respectively. In the 1932 census, schools enrolling 50 to 99 students formed 28% of all schools, whereas in 1930 they were 29.5%. Dr. Crowley stated that one-third of the schools in 1926 had enrollments of 50 to 100 students. [85] The percentage of this group also seems to show a decrease indicating a trend toward larger school enrollments.

In the next higher group of schools, enrolling 100 to 199 students, the 1930 census shows 21.2%, the 1932 census 25.4%, which indicates an upward trend in this group. The next two groups show the same tendency, for schools with 200 to 299 students in 1930 were 6.1% and in 1932, 8.44%; schools enrolling 300 to 499 students in 1930 were 4.4% and in 1932, 5.1%. Schools with 500 to 999 students in 1930 were 2.4%, and in 1932, 2.98%—an increase of one-half of one per cent. In 1930 there were 10 high schools with enrollments 1,000 to 1,999; in 1932 the same 10 high schools were found, but four of the 10 had advanced, three into the group from 2,000 to 2,499 and one into the group from 2,500 to 3,000. Dr. Crowley's study indicated that 3% of the high schools had enrollments exceeding 500 students in 1926; and in 1930 and 1932 as shown in the present study, the percentage had increased to 3.5%. Dr. Crowley showed in his analysis of 1928 statistics on Catholic secondary schools that the median was 74, with the middle 50% ranging from 43 to 154. [85] In the 1932 statistical analysis the mode was the group with 51 to 100 students; the median was 86, and the middle 50% ranged from 44 to 168. Enrollments for 1934-35 stated on vocational questionnaires in this study seem to indicate even more strongly the trend toward larger enrollments in Catholic high schools.

Concerning distribution of students, a study of 1,441 high schools with four-year courses made several years ago showed 165,822 students;

34.7% in the first year, 26.8% in the second year, 20.8% in the third year, and 17.7% in fourth year; in other words, about half of the entering students completed high school work. The Department of Education, National Catholic Welfare Conference, states that Diocesan Superintendents' reports now show an even better distribution. [81] Dr. Crowley quotes public high school figures from the 1924-26 survey showing 37.9% in the first year, 26.7% in the second year, 19.6% in third year, and 15.8% in fourth year. For 1930 public high schools distribution was 55.4% for first year, 27.4% for second year, 20.6% for third year and 16.6% for fourth year; in other words, less than one-third of the entering students completed high school. [82]

The per cent of accreditation of Catholic high schools seems to have remained stationary, indicating that it has grown at the same rate as the number of schools. The 1926 survey showed 65%, and a 1935 study of standardization by Dr. O'Dowd indicated that 66% were accredited to State Departments of Education, State Universities, and the four regional agencies. [84] The present study indicates 72% accredited, the 6% in excess of Dr. O'Dowd's study being accounted for by the inclusion by the writer of high schools accredited by the National Catholic Education Association and Catholic University.

Tables IV and V show the distribution of students to urban and rural areas, and an analysis of the urban areas to indicate their size. Both in numbers of schools in 1932, 81.4%, and in students attending them, 92.5%, Catholic secondary schools are overwhelmingly urban. Public secondary schools are, in number of schools, three-fourths rural, and in number of students, almost three-fourths urban. This situation connotes large high schools, the average for urban public secondary schools being 676 students, and for rural, 87 students. Catholic high schools have an average of 131 students in urban areas, and 43 students in rural areas. As Table V indicates for 1932, 55% of all Catholic secondary students attended schools in 88 cities with population over 100,000. Dr. Crowley indicated that 13 cities with population of over 100,000 had 50% of Catholic secondary school students in 1926. [85] Statistics for 1932, therefore, indicate a wider distribution of students but a continuing trend toward concentration in large cities.

Individual Catholic high school reports for 1932 gave 46,196 as the total number of graduates, which is 16.2% of Catholic high school population for that year. Of these graduates, 27.2% went on to colleges, 15.5% to professional, business, or normal schools. This 43% of students continuing education indicates a decrease of 10% from the 53% shown in a study made in 1926. [81] Public high school figures for 1930 showed that 44.3% of graduates were continuing their education. [82]

From these figures we have seen the distribution of Catholic secondary schools, increases in schools, faculty, and students from 1915 to 1934, percentages of boys', girls' and coeducational schools, and their trends, titles assigned, types of schools and their trends, organization, sizes of high schools and their trends, the mode, median, and range of the middle 50%, distribution of students through the high school years, accreditation, localization in rural and various size of urban areas, numbers of graduates and per cent of students continuing their education in different types of schools. Comparative statistics for public high schools throw these figures into relief.

CHAPTER V

PRESENT STATUS OF VOCATIONAL GUIDANCE IN CATHOLIC HIGH SCHOOLS

The Issue

WE have noted the degree of awareness of the problem of vocational guidance on the part of Catholic educators; we have indicated agencies assisting in the dissemination of the idea of vocational guidance; we have presented previous studies showing evidence of guidance in Catholic high schools; we have demonstrated at length the scope and trend of Catholic secondary education and, comparatively, the trend in public secondary education. We have now to consider how representative is the presentation of the White House Conference, Education and Training, Subcommittee on Vocational Guidance, relative to vocational guidance in Catholic secondary schools. To accomplish this we must compare the philosophy of guidance with the Catholic philosophy of education, then determine how extensively Catholic high schools provide for guidance in the choice of lifework for their rapidly expanding student bodies.

The White House Conference, Education, and Training Subcommittee on Vocational Guidance sent questionnaires to 72 of the 105 dioceses in the United States. Fifteen of these dioceses "indicated that the schools were carrying on one or more vocational guidance activities" as follows:

Discussion of Occupations in Regular Classes	3
Published Studies of Occupations for Use in the Schools	4
Group Conferences to discuss Occupations or Occupational Choices	12
Organized Plans for Student's Individual Conference with Counselor	11
Organized Employment Service	2
Organized Plans for giving Scholarships to Students	9
Follow State Program of Vocational Guidance	1
Diocesan Organization for Vocational Guidance in all High Schools	1
Development of Religious Vocations—in High School Work	2

After presentation of data obtained through the present study, comparisons will be made with items listed above.

Principles of Vocational Guidance Consonant with Principles of Catholic Education

In the Principles of Vocational Guidance outlined by the National Vocational Guidance Association, the statement is made: "Every effort must be made to know the individual, his intelligence, his special abilities, his understanding of work, his health, educational achievement, work experience, temperament, character, interests, and his social and economic situation. These individual differences call for individual attention."

From the Encyclical, or general letter, of Pope XI on the Christian Education of Youth the following quotations will indicate that the aims of Catholic education embrace all factors mentioned above, as well as others: "Christian education takes in the whole aggregate of human life, physical and spiritual, intellectual and moral, individual, domestic and social, not with a view of reducing it in any way but in order to elevate, regulate and perfect it, in accordance with the example and teaching of Christ." Again he says: "Education consists essentially in preparing man for what he must be and for what he must do here below in order to attain the sublime end for which he was created." "It must never be forgotten that the subject of Christian education is man, whole and entire." "Education is essentially a social and not a mere individual activity." "Education is concerned with man as a whole, individually and socially." [89]

Dr. John M. Cooper of Catholic University, Washington, D.C., said: "The choice of lifework and the choice of a lifemate are the two decisions fraught with the greatest consequences to the individual." [86]

In *A Philosophic Basis for Vocational Counsel*, Dr. John M. Wolfe, Diocesan Superintendent, said: "Finding the right work in life has its bearing upon successful living, and in that connection any aid that is given becomes indeed religious. In our times, by the very nature of our social structure the obligation to render aid of this type belongs to the school; it is not a situation that we have created, but nevertheless one that education must meet. A recognition of this philosophy can lead Catholic educators to a more fruitful service to the home, the school, and withal the Church, and meet the challenge successfully that modern conditions are making to the schools. Vocational counsel and many of its extensions are a part of the religious calling, because through them and the right life adjustments that they effect, God's children may be led to their final adjustment to their Creator, which is their ultimate and supreme vocation."[87]

Catholic education and vocational guidance have this aim in common, to develop the student to the fullest extent possible for him—to realize his maximum potentialities. Vocational guidance recognizes group work and individual counseling. This pattern follows the practice of the Church from the earliest times, for corporate worship and individual sacraments and prayer, mental and vocal, satisfy man's need for both social and individual spiritual relationships; this practice carried over into Catholic education. The infinite worth of the individual has always been and is the standard that the Church holds high; this viewpoint motivates all religious and educational work; the development of the individual to his maximum capacity is the corollary of this viewpoint. Vocational guidance is, then, consonant with the aims of Catholic education.

Guidance in Retrospect and Prospect

Catholic education has always had as its primary objective the spiritual development of students, considered always in relation to its physical, social and economic setting. As the Catholic educator viewed each individual student, he encountered a number who thought that they had religious vocations, that is, were "called" to a religious life. These were carefully observed to determine, tentatively, the presence of the necessary will and fitness for Community life, or religious service. Types of religious services, however, are greatly varied. The determination to enter religious life has for its corollary, the selection of the Religious Community preferred, and for this, occupational information and choice are required. It is necessary to know what types of work each Community conducts; one Community has only education as its field of service, while another Community has no restriction on its types of service, and so on. (All Communities, of necessity, include administrative, clerical and maintenance work.)

No figures are available for men Religious, whose types of work are classified under the priesthood, teaching, nursing, social service, clerical, and maintenance. For women Religious we have survey figures of 1933. Ralph G. Hurlin of Russell Sage Foundation reported the total for the United States, 123,304, and the occupational assignment of 105,574. Of these, teaching accounted for 60.5%, and included educational administrators and supervisors, teachers of special subjects, and regular class work, on all levels—elementary, secondary, and collegiate. Nursing accounted for 7.2% and included nursing administrators, and supervisors and instructors of nurses' training schools, nurses, pharmacists, dietitians, and physicians. Administration of the Religious Communities occupied 4.3%, including sisters in charge of institutions and agencies and their more important executive assistants. Social service work—separate from nursing and education—occupied 3.4%. Unfortunately, clerical service was combined with maintenance work in this report, so the exact percentages cannot be given. These two services combined, occupied almost 25% of the Religious. Under clerical work, stenographic and typing work are included, office appliance work and filing, bookkeeping, and all types of accounting. Maintenance included all work of the nature of housekeeping, sewing, laundry, etc. [90]

The proper selection of the Religious Community, therefore, includes occupational choice. In this sense, Catholic educators have always rendered vocational guidance. But, in order to fulfill its objectives of taking into account the entire personality of each individual, Catholic education was obliged to consider the interests of students whose minds were directed toward secular vocations. Capable students were encouraged to continue their education in higher institutions preparing for the desired secular vocation, scholarships were procured by interesting persons who could assist, or by interesting the personnel of a higher school. Every Catholic school which charges tuition has a number—in many cases a fixed percentage—of scholarship students. These scholarships are conferred through competitive examinations, or granted without examination upon recommendation of school officers in lower schools. In some cases entire maintenance is given to deserving students, and under these conditions personal service is asked from the recipient, commensurate with studies and personal strength. Therefore vocational and educational guidance may be said to have existed in an informal state in Catholic high schools since their inception. However, in an informal state it is inevitable that some deserving students are overlooked. Through the organization of guidance plans, the merits and needs of all should have consideration.

With the rapid increase of occupations due to technological changes, came the necessity for knowledge of these vocations and their trends, conditions of work, and requirements, and a consequent necessity for vocational and educational guidance. For students leaving school, these data are a necessity; for those going into higher education, the choice of a goal, even tentative, must precede selection of school or college. To what extent have Catholic high schools adjusted their programs to these modern needs of students; have programs of guidance been initiated, and if so, to what extent; or are these plans in process of formation?

Nation-wide Survey Deemed Necessary

Previous studies on vocational guidance in Catholic high schools, reviewed in Chapter III, were limited to samplings of particular size or type of school, or to geographical areas. A nation-wide survey seemed necessary to determine any significant trend, and this survey, as stated in Chapter I, was undertaken by the writer in 1934. It was felt that the results would serve as background material for the formation of plans for suitable school guidance programs. Chapter I has also indicated that this study was limited to high schools with 25 or more students; elimination of smaller schools was made because they seemed too limited in scope to provide organized guidance work. Through lists forwarded by diocesan superintendents, and by use of the 1932-33 Directory of Catholic Colleges and Schools published by the Department of Education, National Catholic Welfare Conference, 1,648 secondary schools, with 25 or more students each, were discovered in the United States. Before sending questionnaires, it was necessary to secure permission from diocesan superintendents in the 105 dioceses of the United States. One recently-formed diocese replied that it had no secondary schools; two diocesan superintendents refused permission because of the inconvenience of frequent questionnaires; no response to repeated requests could be elicited from 17 dioceses. Out of the 105 dioceses, 81%, or 85 dioceses, co-operated in this study.

Response to the Questionnaire

A copy of the questionnaire forwarded to the 1,648 high schools may be found in the Appendix. School officers in 1,004 schools returned the questionnaire. This number represented 61% of the schools to which questionnaires were sent, and included representation from 48 States and the District of Columbia. The combined enrollments of the 1,004 schools totaled close to 160,000 students. There are thus represented in the present study 61% of the total students in Catholic secondary schools of the United States in 1934.

Geographic Distribution of Respondents

The distribution of these 1,004 schools according to geographic areas is reported in Table VIII. The eight groupings of states are:

New England	*Middle Atlantic*	*South Atlantic*	*South Central*
Connecticut	New Jersey	Delaware	Alabama
Maine	New York	Dist. of Columbia	Arkansas
Massachusetts	Pennsylvania	Florida	Kentucky
New Hampshire		Georgia	Louisiana
Rhode Island		Maryland	Mississippi
Vermont		North Carolina	Oklahoma
		South Carolina	Tennessee
		Virginia	Texas
		West Virginia	

North Central (Great Lakes)	*North Central* (Prairie)	*Plateau*	*Pacific*
Illinois	Iowa	Arizona	California
Indiana	Kansas	Colorado	Oregon
Ohio	Missouri	Idaho	Washington
Michigan	Nebraska	Montana	
Minnesota	North Dakota	Nevada	
Wisconsin	South Dakota	New Mexico	
		Utah	
		Wyoming	

Examination of the data of Table VIII reveals that the largest proportion of Catholic high schools are located in the North Central states, Great Lake region, and that this region contributed the largest propor-

TABLE VIII

NUMBER OF SCHOOLS IN EIGHT SECTIONS OF THE UNITED STATES WHICH FURNISHED
DATA FOR THIS STUDY

Section	All High Schools 1932	High Schools Sent Questionnaires No.	%	High Schools Returning Questionnaires No.	%	% of Response
New England............	172	138	80	73	53	7.3
Middle Atlantic.........	508	370	72.8	244	66	24.3
South Atlantic..........	122	99	81	47	50	4.7
South Central............	251	189	75.3	93	50	9.3
North Central (Great Lakes)...............	545	486	90	306	63	30.5
North Central (Prairie)..	299	221	74	157	71	15.6
Plateau................	54	50	90.2	37	74	3.7
Pacific.................	122	96	78.7	47	50	4.7

tion of respondents (30.5%) since it received the largest number of
questionnaires. The Middle Atlantic states rank second in number of
secondary schools, in schools which received questionnaires, and in
responses (24.3%). It will be observed that almost 55% of the returned questionnaires were submitted by schools in these two geographic areas. The Prairie group of the North Central states is third in
number of schools, of those receiving questionnaires and of respondents
(15.6%). Nine per cent (9.3%) of replies were contributed by the
South Central states, while a smaller proportion (7.3%) came from the
New England states. Two groups of states, the South Atlantic and the
Pacific states, supplied equal percentages of schools responding
(4.7%). The Plateau states submitted the smallest proportion of replies (3.7%). It is quite obvious that the groups of states contributed
to the total number of high schools in 1932, and to the responses to this
study in the same ranking order. If we consider the percentage return
of questionnaires sent, the Plateau and the Prairie group of North Central states contributed a far greater return on questionnaires sent than
groups with larger numbers of schools. We may recall at this point that
not all dioceses co-operated in this study—which may account for many
inconsistencies.

Size of Communities Represented in This Study

A consideration of Table IX relative to the percentage of schools in
this study, 393, which are located in cities over 100,000 population,

TABLE IX

DISTRIBUTION OF 1,004 CATHOLIC HIGH SCHOOLS IN THIS STUDY IN CITIES OF VARIOUS
SIZES, AND RURAL AREAS, COMPARED WITH DISTRIBUTION OF ALL CATHOLIC HIGH SCHOOLS,
1932

Section	Cities Over 100,000	Cities 99,999 to 30,000	Cities 29,999 to 10,000	Cities 9,999 to 2,500	Rural Under 2,500	No.	Total %
New England.....	25	21	16	7	4	73	7.2
Middle Atlantic ..	131	32	40	24	17	244	24.3
South Atlantic....	25	9	3	5	5	47	4.7
South Central.....	28	17	18	14	16	93	9.3
North Central (Great Lakes)..	127	42	45	38	54	306	30.5
North Central (Prairie).......	25	16	25	24	67	157	15.6
Plateau..........	5	6	12	13	1	37	3.7
Pacific...........	27	8	4	1	7	47	4.7
Total............	393 (39.1%)	151 (15%)	163 (16.3%)	126 (12.6%)	171 (17%)	1,004	100
All Catholic High Schools—1932..	738 (35.6%)	320 (15.5%)	332 (16%)	297 (14.3%)	386 (18.6%)	2,073	100
Difference in This Study..........	+3.5%	−.5%	+.3%	−1.7%	−1.6%		0

will reveal a slightly larger per cent (3.5%) than is found in all Catholic high schools for 1932, or 738. This increase is so small that the
distribution may be considered typical. Cities of 30,000 to 99,999 population contributed 15% of the schools, 151 considered in this study,
and 15.5% of all Catholic high schools in 1932, 320,—a difference of
one-half of one per cent. In the next group of cities, 163, which have
a population of 10,000 to 29,999, respondents to the questionnaire furnished 16.3% of the total, whereas the 332 schools in 1932 formed 16%
of all high schools, a difference of three-tenths of one per cent. Cities
in the lowest class, with population 2,500 to 9,999, showed a decrease
of 1.7% in the percentage of 126 schools in this study (12.6%) as compared with the percentage of the 297 schools (14.3%) contributed to
the total number of Catholic high schools 1932. One hundred and
seventy-one schools in rural areas, i.e., under 2,500 population, showed
a decrease of 1.6% for those who contributed to this study as compared
with those 386 schools in the total of Catholic high schools, 1932—the
exact percentages being 17% and 18%, respectively. The distribution
of schools in this study may therefore be considered typical of the Cath-

olic high school distribution in 1932 relative to the size of civic communities in which Catholic high schools were located.

Types of High Schools and Classification of Students Contributing to This Study

A consideration of the types of schools and classifications of student bodies which contributed to this study, seems necessary at this point. Table X supplies these data.

TABLE X

<small>TYPES OF HIGH SCHOOLS AND CLASSIFICATIONS OF STUDENTS REPRESENTED IN STUDY, COMPARED WITH ALL CATHOLIC HIGH SCHOOLS IN UNITED STATES, 1932</small>

Types of High Schools	Boys	Girls	Coeducational	Total in This Study No.	%	Total in U. S. 1932 No.	%
Central..........	37	39	48	124	12.35	215	10.4
Parochial........	18	87	381	486	48.4	1,096	52.9
Independent......	101	241	52	394	39.25	762	36.7
Total in Study....	156	367	481	1,004	100		
	(15.54%)	(36.56%)	(47.9%)				
Total High Schools 1932..........	265 (12.8%)	695 (33.53%)	1,113 (53.67%)	...	...	2,073	100

The figures of Table X indicate that central and private or independent high schools contributed a greater percentage, and parochial high schools a lesser percentage to this study than they did to the total high schools in 1932, but the maximum difference in percentage (4.5%) does not preclude the statement that the distribution as to type is typical of all Catholic high schools.

The 156 boys' high schools contributed 2.74% more to this study than to the total of high schools—265; the 367 girls' high schools also contributed 3.03% more to this study than the 695 girls' high schools to the total of high schools, while the 481 coeducational schools contributed 5.77% less to the study than the 1,113 schools did to the total high schools in 1932. The distribution may therefore be considered typical of all Catholic high schools relative to classification of student bodies.

High Schools in the Study Typical in Size

In 1932 Catholic high schools were classified by the writer in seven groups, according to size: those with fewer than 25 students; with

TABLE XI

ENROLLMENTS OF HIGH SCHOOLS IN THIS STUDY COMPARED WITH ALL CATHOLIC
HIGH SCHOOLS, 1932

Enrollment of High Schools	This Study		All Catholic High Schools		Difference Based on 1,861 High Schools (i.e., on 2,073 — 212 High Schools with Fewer than 25 Students)
	No.	%	No.	%	
Under 25.........	...	...	212	...	....
25– 99.......	494	49.2	982	52.8	−3.6%
100– 199.......	291	29.0	527	28.3	+0.7
200– 499.......	167	16.6	281	15.1	+1.5
500– 999.......	42	4.2	61	3.2	+1.0
1,000–1,999.......	7	0.7	6	0.4	+0.3
2,000–3,000.......	3	0.3	4	0.2	+0.1
	1,004	100	2,073	100	0

25 to 99 students; with 100 to 199 students; with 200 to 499 students; with 500 to 999 students; with 1,000 to 1,999 students; and with 2,000 to 3,000 students. In this study, high schools were divided in the same way, but schools with fewer than 25 students were omitted. In computing percentages of the 1932 groups comparable with those in this study, the total number of high schools less the 212 schools having fewer than 25 students was used as the basis, since it was believed this would give a truer picture for comparison.

Table XI shows that only 494 schools, 49.2%, of the Catholic high schools considered in this study had students numbering from 25 to 99 students; whereas 52.8% of all Catholic high schools in 1932 is represented by the 982 schools, a negative difference of 3.6%. This difference is so slight, however, that it does not affect the close similarity of percentages. High schools with 100 to 199 students in this study number 291, or 29%; in this same group 527 schools (28.3%) were found in the total of high schools, 1932, a positive difference of 0.7%; this group also may be considered typical. In this study high schools with students from 200 to 499 number 167 or 16.6%; in all high schools, 1932, high schools of this size number 281 or 15.1%, a positive difference of 1.5%, indicating that schools of this size are represented to a slightly greater degree in this study than they are in the total of high schools, 1932. In the next group of high schools with students from 500 to 999, 42 are represented in this study (4.2%), whereas in the total of high schools, 1932, schools of this size are 61 in number (3.2%), again a positive difference of 1%, showing a representation in this study slightly greater than in all high schools, 1932. Seven high schools with students from 1,000 to 1,999 are found in this study—0.7%; in the total of high schools, 1932, six high schools of this size are shown— 0.4%; a postive difference of 0.3% shows this group somewhat better represented in this study. In the group of Catholic high schools with the largest enrollments—from 2,000 to 3,000 students—three are represented in this study, or 0.3%; in the total of high schools, 1932, four are shown, or 0.2%; this group is then represented to a slightly greater degree (0.1%) in this study than in the total high schools, 1932. In the matter of size of schools, therefore, the writer feels that this study is typical of Catholic high schools, since the maximum variation is 0.6%.

Schools Contributing to This Study Are Typical of Catholic High Schools

Since the high schools contributing to this study seem comparable to Catholic high schools relative to geographical distribution, to distribution to various size cities and rural areas, to types of high schools and classification of students and to sizes of high schools, these 1,004 secondary schools may be said to be typical of Catholic high schools in the United States.

Responses to the Questionnaire

We have indicated in Chapter I that 1,004 school officers of the 1,648 sent questionnaires responded and that the enrollment ranged from 25 to 2,970. Boys' schools seem to have larger enrollments than the girls', yet girls' schools monopolize the very largest classification; in the smaller sized high schools, girls' schools and the coeducational seem almost equal.

Desire for a large return led the investigator to urge in the letter accompanying the questionnaire that the school officer check question 3 and return the form, if there were no guidance activities in the school. Very quickly the error was perceived. Many schools who are known to provide to a fair degree for student guidance understood that only a completely organized program of guidance was intended in the response, and checked "No." A postscript was then appended to the letter asking school officials to check any activities they had in order to receive credit for them, and a more representative response was the result.

Interest in Guidance and Stimuli

Only five respondents expressed themselves not interested in vocational guidance, one saying specifically, "not as an organized course." Eight hundred and thirteen school officers expressed themselves interested, which is more than 81% of school officers forwarding questionnaires. When the source of interest was probed through question 2, the greater number of educators—664—expressed themselves as interested, "through observing the need for guidance"; this is 66.13% of all respondents. The second stimulus to interest, "through your own reading," yielded 286 (28.48%) of all responding. Many educators checked two sources of their interest, and these two, "observing the need for guidance" and "through your own reading" were used together most frequently. Speakers or addresses on guidance proved the stimuli in the case of 162 school officers (16.1%) of those responding. The National Catholic Education Association was named as the source of interest in 69 cases, state requirements in 42 cases, and diocesan requirements in 5 cases—a total of 1,228 responses. These are indicated in Table XII.

TABLE XII

EDUCATORS EXPRESSING THEMSELVES INTERESTED, AND STIMULI TO INTEREST*
Educators interested—813; Not interested—5; Total responding—818

Stimulus	No. Responses
"Through observing the need for guidance"	664
"Through your own reading"	286
"Through speakers"	162
"Through National Catholic Education Association"	69
"Through state requirements"	42
"Through diocesan requirements"	5
Total responses	1,228

* More than one source of stimulus was checked by many.

The wish to discover stimuli resulting in interest had its origin in the hope that these sources might be utilized in disseminating the idea of guidance. Since the source has proved basic, it seems only necessary to satisfy it by suggesting ways and means of introducing guidance more widely into schools, or of making known plans already in use, and therefore feasible.

Extent of Present Guidance Work

Nine hundred sixteen (916) school officers responded to question 3, "Do you provide vocational guidance for students in your school?" Four hundred and ninety-eight (498) or 49.6% stated that they provided vocational guidance; 314 (31.3%) stated that they did not; and 104 (10.3%) wrote in the word "informally"; while 88 (8.8%) did not respond. Table XIII presents these figures.

TABLE XIII

CATHOLIC SECONDARY SCHOOLS PROVIDING VOCATIONAL GUIDANCE

Type of Provision	Number of Schools	Per Cent of All Respondents	Per Cent of All Catholic High Schools, 1932
Providing vocational guidance.........	498	49.6%	26.7%
Providing informal guidance...........	104	10.3	5.5
Do not provide guidance..............	314	31.3	16.9
No response.........................	88	8.8	4.6
Total.........................	916	91.0	53.7

Inaugurating Work in High Schools

Question 4 was divided into three parts: A. "In what year did you begin any work of this kind in your school?" Dates of inception were divided into three groups, those schools which reported beginning work in the decade 1910-1920, of which there were 15; those which stated they began in the decade 1920-1930, a total of 85 schools; and the period 1930-1934, in which 159 schools stated that they had begun work. This total of 259 schools reporting dates of inception shows that the period 1930-1934 saw a great growth of guidance in Catholic high schools, since the total for that period is 150% of all schools which stated that they had begun work in the decades 1910-1920 and 1920-1930. Table XIV summarizes these data.

If so many Catholic educators have observed the need for guidance, they should be alert to devise opportunities for utilizing plans which seem adapted for their particular schools. No one plan can be suggested which is adaptable for all schools, but keen observation and ingenuity are needed both in initiating and maintaining a program.

TABLE XIV

CALENDAR YEARS AND SCHOOL YEARS IN WHICH VOCATIONAL GUIDANCE WAS BEGUN
IN CATHOLIC HIGH SCHOOLS

Calendar Year	Number
1910–1920	15
1920–1930	85
1930–1934	159
Total schools reporting	259

School Year	Number
7th grade	18 (4.8%)
8th grade	31 (7.9%)
9th grade	200 (50%)
10th grade	37 (9%)
11th grade	41 (10.2%)
12th grade	48 (12%)
7th and 8th grades	5 (1.2%)
9th and 10th grades	3 (0.7%)
9th and 11th grades	2 (0.5%)
8th and 12th grades	1 (0.2%)
10th, 11th, and 12th grades	2 (0.5%)
All grades in 4-year High School	11 (3%)
Total schools reporting	409 (100%)

To the second and third parts of this fourth question: "In what year of school did you begin?" and "Why did you choose this grade?" 409 schools responded. Fifty per cent of these schools reporting began work in the ninth grade; 12% in the senior year of high school, 10% in the junior year; 9% in the sophomore year; and 3% in all years of high school. The remaining 16% was divided among various combinations of years, including junior high school years. Where a change in grade had been made, an earlier year was chosen in each case. Reasons for choosing the particular location for vocational guidance work were listed as follows:

Seventh and Eighth Grades

Pupils begin to think about the future.
Begin to think about choosing.
Some are most receptive to the idea.
Some think seriously about it.
To clarify interests and try out results in high school.

Ninth Grade

Pupils are more interested then.
Realize the necessity for it.
Old enough to appreciate such guidance.
To survey occupations in preparation for choice.
To select subjects desired.

Ninth Grade (Cont.)

To choose correct course.
To provide goal for effort.
Objectives for work.
Have four years to work with student.
Form some outlook on life.
Felt 12th grade was too late.
Pupils welcomed it.
Never too soon to begin.
Advisable to direct attention.
Students begin to think of future then.
Adolescence.
Mature enough to profit from suggestions.
Best to watch developments.
Why not?
To retain students in school.
To give as broad a view as possible as early as possible.

Tenth Grade

Development at that age.
Attitudes are most marked.

Tenth Grade (Cont.)

So many awaken to responsibilities and possibilities.
Some leave high school then.
To select courses and electives.

Eleventh Grade

Branch out *after* required subjects.
Necessity for educational guidance.
Stabilize ideas of students.
More mature students.
Know students better, and students know their own minds better.
Better able to understand the need for study and guidance.

Twelfth Grade

The need is most pressing then.
Last year in high school.
Last year of school for many.
More practical interest.
Students do a little more thinking.
Pupils are more mature.
Many think of choosing their life-work.
Just previous to college.

This preferential placing of the class in guidance in the ninth grade corresponds with Table VIII of Koos and Kefauver's *Guidance in Secondary Schools,* which indicates that more than 50% of junior high school guidance classes were placed in the ninth grade as well as almost 75% of occupational courses in four-year high schools. The trend of practice, then, favors the ninth grade in public and Catholic schools.

To question 5, "Was work begun on an informal basis, or with a class organized?" 580 schools replied. Of these 451—78% of those reporting—had begun work informally; whether it was individual or group work was not indicated. Two hundred and ninety-eight school officers answered "yes" to question 6, which asked, "Have you changed from the informal to the more organized form, i.e., in a class for guidance, studying occupations, vocational civics, or English themes on the subject, or has the work been integrated with other classes, and if so, with which ones?" Some schools checked two or more of these. The more organized form consisted of a class for guidance in 39 schools; of vocational civics in 100 schools; of English themes on occupations in 152 schools; of correlation with all subjects in 5 schools; and with other specifically mentioned subjects in 45 schools. Data are shown in Table XV.

TABLE XV

MANNER OF INITIATING GUIDANCE PROGRAM; AND CHANGE TO ORGANIZED FORM

	No.	%
Began guidance program informally	451	78
Began guidance program with organized class	129	22
Total reporting	580	
Class for guidance	39	
Vocational civics	100	
English themes on occupations	152	
Correlated guidance with all subjects	5	
Correlated guidance with specific subjects	45	
	(341)*	
Total reporting	298	

* Percentages cannot be computed because some schools checked more than one.

TABLE XVI

PERSONNEL USED IN INITIATING GUIDANCE IN CATHOLIC HIGH SCHOOLS

	No.	%
Used all teachers	115	22
Used home-room teachers	235	45
Used selected teachers	169	32
Total reporting	521	

The investigator was interested in guidance personnel included, and asked question 8, "In beginning guidance were all teachers used, or home-room teachers or selected teachers?" Table XVI presents data reported. When guidance plans are made, the personnel included may mean the success or the failure of the plan. The history of guidance in public high schools shows many instances of failure because all faculty were not convinced, and included in the making of plans. Trained vocational counselors, subject teachers, home-room teachers—all must assist in making the plan a success, for even with a trained specialist as guidance director it is the teachers who will do at least half of the work. In small schools with four to eight teachers, each teacher plays a very important part in the guidance scheme; but in larger schools, to name all teachers as part of the guidance personnel reminds the writer of a university professor who responded to a "bluffing answer," "Perfectly true, perfectly general, and perfectly meaningless." What is everyone's work is no one's work. Personnel work has its requirements just as all professional work has, and not everyone meets the requirements. To spread thin over a large faculty the responsibility for guidance is to insure its failure.

Replies to question 8 were sent by 521 school officers; 22% of those reporting, 115, used all teachers in beginning vocational guidance work; 235 or 45% used home-room teachers and 32% or 169 schools used selected teachers. It is noteworthy that nearly one-half of the school officers reporting had used home-room teachers, which argues very strongly for the inclusion of guidance in the courses of teachers colleges as required courses, and also in other colleges offering courses in education. This guidance viewpoint on the part of the teacher is essential to insure the proper development of each individual pupil.

Increase in Time Devoted to Guidance

The writer was interested also in the reaction to guidance after it had been begun in a school, so asked in question 9, "Have you increased the time given to guidance, and why?" Three hundred and twenty-one school officers reported on this question; of this number 101 or almost 31% stated that they had increased the time, and almost 70% stated that they had not increased time devoted to guidance. The negative responses to this question do not mean a lack of interest in guidance or a lack of faith in its efficacy; many who answered that they had not increased the time given to guidance stated as the reason that they had provided sufficient time in setting up the program. Replies to question 9 are shown in Table XVII.

Reasons for not increasing time allotted to guidance activities were reviewed and were found to center around lack of time, demands of the curriculum and lack of trained teachers. A few responded that it was not necessary in their opinion, and one school officer felt that the results did not justify increasing the time. From the tone of the response, the cause seemed to be in the administration. In reasons given

TABLE XVII

"Increased Time Devoted to Vocational Guidance?"

	No.	%
Yes	101	31
No	220	69
Total schools reporting	321	100

for increasing time devoted to guidance all testify to a new motivation in the students, and greater results in all work. To the writer it appears that in public schools as well as in Catholic high schools, an individual teacher or administrator is often the key to effective guidance, and to increase of interest. With his departure or advent effective guidance ebbs or flows. Some reasons advanced to account for increasing time devoted to vocational guidance were:

Found it paid
Saw the need
Interest of students
Much needed
Better results
See the necessity
Progress
Requires more time
Children happier
To direct ideas

Because it seemed helpful
Greater service rendered
Credit is now given
Believe in its importance
Because of increased enrollment
Because competition is so keen
Because of keen interest and practical results
Present-day importance
More interest manifested
Organization of youth

To cover all phases of vocational and educational guidance

Devices Used in Vocational Guidance

A knowledge of the devices or techniques used to accomplish guidance may be gained from Table XVIII. Questions 6 and 7 specifically named these, asking school officers to check techniques used in that particular school. Question 6 also afforded opportunity for school officers to write in subjects with which vocational guidance was correlated. We note from Table XVIII that the chief devices used by schools in this study were, in rank: Students' interviews with teachers and school officers, 229; Assembly talks by representatives of vocations, 172; Assembly talks by teachers and school officers, 138; Referring students to vocational literature, 132; and Follow-up of graduates, 109. Occupational observation and field-trips were few—51, the small number being due, no doubt, to the closing of industries be-cause of economic conditions. Case studies of student's problems, 88, offered opportunity for students to see difficulties and possible solutions in type cases, a method which should assist them in ana-lyzing their own problems. The writer regards the number of schools reporting physical examinations, 36, totally inadequate. All schools need this service to assist vocational counselors in deciding on the feasibility of a vocation chosen by a student, so as to confirm the pos-sibility or preclude the student's entrance into the desired vocation.

TABLE XVIII

TECHNIQUES USED IN CATHOLIC HIGH SCHOOLS IN VOCATIONAL GUIDANCE

	High Schools in This Study	
	No.	%
Assembly talks by Representatives of vocations	172	17
Student interviews with Representatives of vocations	71	7
Assembly talks by teachers or school officers	138	13
Student interviews with teachers and school officers	229	22
Case studies of students' problems	88	8
Occupational observation and field trips	51	3
Clubs	57	5
Meetings after school	38	3
Follow-up of graduates	109	10
Follow-up of drop-outs	28	2
Physical examination	36	3
Follow-up of bright students	37	3
Follow-up of failing students	50	5
Referring students to vocational literature	132	13
Schools using tests:		
Intelligence	340	34
Aptitude	98	9
Achievement	265	26
Mechanical ability	26	2
Personnel inventory	48	4
Character study and practice	172	17%

Clubs as a Guidance Device

The use of clubs in vocational guidance work was reported by 57 schools, 5.6%. This low percentage seems to indicate that school offi-cers do not recognize the guidance values inherent in school clubs. To observe the student in action in his club activities and human rela-tionships is most necessary for a counselor in "learning the student"; to spur on students to self-reliance, initiative, and group participation, clubs are invaluable; to use clubs as a means for surveying occupations related to the club's interests is a most satisfactory method of conveying occupational information.

Meetings after school for discussion of occupational interests were used by 38 schools. These meetings took the place of clubs or classes in occupations, since time was lacking in the school schedule. In a few cases they were used by teachers to convince school administrators that students were interested in vocational guidance, so interested that they would give up recreation time for it. It proved the issue in some cases, and time was allotted on the school schedule.

Follow-up of Students

Emphasis seems to have been placed upon the follow-up of failing students rather than of the bright, who should be encouraged to take the leadership; 24% more follow-up was reported of failing students than of the bright. The questionnaire response to this technique was not at all satisfactory in the opinion of the investigator. School officers have not realized the possibilities inherent in a discussion between counselor and student relative to his achievement and his capability. The topic of such an interview is concrete and interesting to the student. If the development of the individual to his capacity is the goal of guidance, then achievement—factual and potential—is the very "stuff" of which guidance is made.

Vocational Literature

Referring students to vocational literature as a source of information on occupations was used as a guidance technique in 132 schools (13%). Since public libraries are able to assist students with such literature, including bibliographies on occupations and current periodicals carrying articles on trends in occupations, this percentage seems low. Guidance should be considered a continuous process, and therefore a technique should be acquired by the student to enable him at all times to gain reliable information on prospective occupations. The literature of guidance and library sources of information are absolutely necesary in guidance; the habit of using such sources should be acquired by the student as an essential of his technique for continuous self-guidance.

Objective Means of Knowing Students

The use of objective tests in vocational guidance is a recognized procedure. While intelligence tests play the leading role, achievement tests follow second in extent of use. More than one-third of the Catholic schools responding—340 or 34%—used intelligence tests, while 265 or 26% stated that achievement tests were in use in those schools. Aptitude tests had been used in 98 schools, almost 10%, but responses indicated that school officers using them were dissatisfied with them, considering that they contributed little or nothing to the counselor's knowledge of the students' abilities. Personal inventories were used in 48 schools, less than 5% of the respondents. Tests of mechanical ability were in use in 26 schools, about 2.5% of those responding. Tests for character study and practice were used in 172 schools, or 17%.

The Class in Occupations

Three times in the questionnaire the class in occupations was mentioned: in question 7 among many devices; in questions 10, 11, and 12, from the administrative viewpoint, data were requested relative to date of introducing the work and the school year, and whether or not the year of school had been changed and why, whether it was a required subject, whether credit was given, and the texts and references used; in question 25 the inquiry concerned the content of the course, i.e., whether all occupations were presented, or only local ones.

Since a knowledge of the fields of occupation, including information about opening of new opportunities, and possible decline and change in others, is a preliminary to choice of occupation, the dissemination of occupational information is of prime importance to secondary school students. From the writer's knowledge of vocational guidance in high schools, this phase has received least attention. Separation of the inquiries concerning the class in occupations was intended to lend emphasis to this project.

A knowledge of the frequency of use of the occupations class as a device in vocational guidance may be gained from Table XIX. About 10%, or 101 schools, offered classes in occupations, 38 requiring the work, and 35 offering it as an elective; 28 schools did not return data. Of the 38 schools requiring the course, 29 gave one credit, three two credits, three offered one-half credit, and three gave no credit. Of the

35 schools offering the work as an elective, 18 schools gave one credit, or one-half unit, four schools gave two credits, four schools gave one-half credit, and nine schools gave no credit. Almost 45% of the schools reporting extended the course in occupations over two to four years, with a wide variety of groupings of the years. However, only 71% of schools reporting the course indicated in what year it was given.

TABLE XIX

CATHOLIC HIGH SCHOOLS OFFERING COURSES IN OCCUPATIONS, CREDIT GRANTED, AND LOCATION IN HIGH SCHOOL

	Number
Offer Course in Occupations	101
Required Course	38
No credit	3
Credit given, ¼ unit	3
Credit given, ½ unit	29
Credit given, 1 unit	3
Elective Course	35
No credit	9
Credit given, ¼ unit	4
Credit given, ½ unit	18
Credit given, 1 unit	4
Schools not reporting	28
9th grade course in occupations	18
10th grade course in occupations	4
11th grade course in occupations	2
12th grade course in occupations	15
9th and 10th grades course in occupations	7
10th and 11th grades course in occupations	3
11th and 12th grades course in occupations	10
9th, 10th, 11th grades course in occupations	22
9th and 12th grades course in occupations	1
10th, 11th, and 12th grades course in occupations	1
9th, 10th, 11th, 12th grades course in occupations	9
Schools reporting	72
Offer survey of all occupations	109
Offer survey of local occupations only	33
Schools reporting	142

Question 25 asked whether all occupations were included, and almost 77% of the schools reporting, 109, replied in the affirmative, while 23%, 33, presented only local occupations. This total of schools reporting, 142, represents a 40% increase over the schools reporting a class in occupations elsewhere. This discrepancy possibly may be accounted for by surveys of vocations being included in classes for guidance, vocational civics, English classes, or any other devices employed and mentioned in questions 6 or 7. To the inquiry in question 12, relative to texts and references in use, many lengthy lists were returned. No tabulation could be made because of the variety in both texts and references, except in states which had recommended texts.

Interviews with Students

Question 23 asked: "Do students have interviews—freshman, sophomore, junior, or senior years?" repeating the item of question 7 to which 229 school officers responded affirmatively. To the inquiry in question 23, as shown in Table XX, 296 school officers, 29%, replied in the affirmative, and of these almost one-half interviewed all students, 49%. In five schools freshmen only had interviews, less than 2%; 7 school officers interviewed only sophomores—a trifle over 2%; juniors only were interviewed in 6% of the schools, 18; seniors only in 21%, 62; while 60 schools, 20%, did not indicate the classes which had interviews. Interpreted, this means that in almost 15% of the Catholic high schools responding, interviews are held with all the students.

TABLE XX

CATHOLIC HIGH SCHOOLS OFFERING COUNSELING INTERVIEWS TO STUDENTS

	Schools in This Study	
	No.	%
Freshmen	5	2
Sophomores	7	2
Juniors	18	6
Seniors	62	21
All classes	144	49
Years not indicated	60	20
Schools reporting	296	

The responses to question 24, "How many interviews, usually, in the student's high school life?" were so widely varied, that tabulation is not possible. They ranged from the vague and unorganized to the definite "4 to 10." Personnel work cannot be reduced to a matter of statistics, but an average number, it seemed, should have emerged in practice. The desire not to reduce the human equation to a mathematical fixity may be very commendable, but the investigator had hoped for an expression of the average number of interviews which were found necessary or helpful. If decision must be made between granting interviews or recording them, by all means the choice should be to grant or hold an interview.

Surveys of Local Employment and Community Co-operation

In asking question 26 relative to surveys of local employment, co-operation with community agencies, and current reports forwarded to school offices, the investigator desired to discover counselors' knowledge of federal, state, or city surveys. In 10% of the schools replying, as shown in Table XXI, responses indicated a knowledge of such surveys. Many school officials understood that it was incumbent on them to make a survey of this sort, and in 14 instances the officials, students, or alumni of the school had made it; firms and professional people had made it in 7 cases, chambers of commerce in 5 instances, clubs in 2 cases, and state and federal agencies in 2 instances. Of community agencies co-operating, the chamber of commerce was named 15 times, school officials were mentioned 6 times, local business agencies 5 times, and clubs twice.

TABLE XXI

City Occupational Surveys, and Agencies Co-operating

	School Officers
Knowledge of federal, state, or city surveys	103
School officials, students, or alumni, making survey	14
Firms and professional people making survey	7
Chambers of commerce making survey	5
Clubs making survey	2
State and federal agencies making survey	2
Community agencies co-operating	
Chamber of Commerce named—times	15
School officials named—times	6
Local business agencies	5
Clubs	2

Occupational employment information kept up-to-date in 37 schools by files controlled by the principal's secretary—3.6% of schools responding to this study.

Placement and Follow-up in Guidance

Relative to placement of students in positions or tryout work, question 29 asked, "Do counselors make placement of students?" Table XXII presents results.

One hundred and fifty of the schools, 15%, stated that they regularly placed students, but that such placement was almost impossible just then because of industrial and business conditions. With adjustment to better economic conditions, counselors expressed themselves ready to resume placement work.

In response to question 30, "Do counselors follow-up the employed to see the success of the student in the work or in that particular place of work?" follow-up of students placed was reported by 137 schools, 13%. Alumni or alumnae were organized to assist in guidance, i.e., for informative assistance and field trips as well as in employment—in 95 schools—about 9% of schools responding. Assistance to alumni was recorded by 371 schools—37%, in response to question 31, indicating an active interest in welfare of graduates. This assistance took the form of securing scholarships for higher education, and also securing employment. Table XXII records these figures.

TABLE XXII

CATHOLIC HIGH SCHOOLS OFFERING PLACEMENT AND FOLLOW-UP IN GUIDANCE

	Schools in This Study	
Question	No.	%
29. School officers making placement............................	150	15
30. Follow-up of students placed...............................	137	13
31. Alumni organized to assist students........................	95	9.4
33. Counselors assist alumni—placements, etc..................	371	37

Guidance Records

Records necessary for continuity of guidance were kept by 99 schools—less than 10%—as indicated in Table XXIII.

TABLE XXIII

CATHOLIC HIGH SCHOOLS KEEPING STUDENT RECORDS FOR GUIDANCE PURPOSES

	Schools in This Study	
	No.	%
Student guidance records kept................................	99	9.5
Records centralized for faculty use..........................	60	5.8

Question 28 also asked concerning centralization of these cumulative records for use by the faculty, and 60 schools replied in the affirmative, 9 in the negative.

Educational Guidance

Guidance concerning choice of subjects in high school was presupposed by the investigator in connection with the student's choice of occupation, hence no specific mention was made of it. Question 32, however, asked concerning assistance given relative to choice of college or technical school, and 528 schools—52%—responded in the affirmative. No request was made concerning methods or extent of the assistance given, but merely the fact of the school's rendering assistance in choice of the school for further education.

Administration of Guidance

Questions 13 to 22 inclusive, related to administration of the vocational guidance work. Table XXIV tabulates the replies to these questions. It is noteworthy, as this table shows, that 453 principals acted as counselor, 45% of schools responding. In 227 schools other school officers acted as counselor, the vice-principal being named many times; counselors were found in 160 schools, 16% of those responding, and of these 23 were giving full time to counseling; 118 of them were teachers who had prepared through reading for counseling, and 110 had had special training for counseling. In reply to question 19, 177 stated that they had "in-service training." This number is 17 in excess of those schools that reported counselors. This discrepancy may be accounted for by the including of school officers serving as counselors who had not had special training, but had read and gained confidence by practice—the trial and error plan. The counselor was a member of a Religious Community in 279 cases. This number also is in excess of the 160 counselors recorded, and must include principals, and other school officers serving as counselors. In 101 schools a priest was counselor.

One counselor each attended the following: University of Dayton, Ohio; DePaul University, Chicago; European Universities; University of Montreal; New Jersey Teachers' College; Marygrove, Detroit; Simmons College, Boston; Stanford, Palo Alto; Villanova, Pa.; Catholic University and Johns Hopkins; Catholic University and Louvain; Columbia and Fordham; Harvard and Notre Dame.

Replies to question 17, relative to the time given to counselor's duties by part-time counselors, varied from "Teach two classes a day, and give the remainder of the day to counselor's duties" to "a few hours a week."

TABLE XXIV

School Officers Serving as Counselor in Catholic High Schools

Question	Schools in This Study No.	%
13. Principal acts as counselor	453	45
14. Other school officer acts as counselor	227	22
15. Schools having counselors	160	16
16. Full time to counseling	23	2
17. Counselor was a teacher who prepared for counseling	118	11
18. Counselor has had special training	110	11
19. "In-service training"	177	17
20. Counselor is a member of a Religious Community	279	27
21. Counselor is a priest	101	10

Subjects Taught by Part-Time Counselors

Question	Schools in This Study
16. Religion	70
English	29
Social Studies and Sociology	16
Science	6
Languages, Ancient and Modern	12
Subjects Not Named	37
Schools reporting	170

Title Assigned to Counselor

15. Student counselor	17
Student adviser	7
Counselor	7
Vocational counselor and vocational guide	3
Moderator of Sodality	5
Schools reporting	39

Colleges in Which Counselors Secured Special Training

	Counselors
20. Catholic University	7
Columbia University	5
Fordham University	3
Loyola University of the North, Chicago	2
Loyola University of the South, New Orleans	2
Notre Dame University	6
St. Louis University	7
Jesuit Colleges (not named)	6
University of Minnesota	3
University of Pennsylvania	3
Marquette University	2
Colleges (not named)	5

Question 22 asked regarding the relation of the counselor to advisers for classes, deans and others. The following were a few of the responses:

Adviser	Co-operator	Director of Co-operation	"On Parallel"
"Close"	Correlate	Executive Officer	President of School Board
Colaborer	Dean	Gives Informal Talks	Supervisor
Consultor	Director	Joins in Conference	Vice-Principal

Members of Religious Communities as Counselors

The question has arisen in educational conferences whether members of Religious Communities, particularly women, can be vocational counselors, and the decision has been reached that they can be, that the idea is perfectly feasible, and recommended. The origin of the idea seemed to be the opinion that women enter Religious Communities so young and inexperienced that they have no idea of the business world, knowing only a home world and the convent, and therefore they cannot give information relative to occupational conditions and problems. From history we know that women superiors of convents managed convent finances, property, erection of buildings, and every type of training schools centuries before the modern woman emerged into the business world. In order to determine just how experienced Religious women were before they entered the convent, the investigator made a survey of two Religious Communities for women. The findings are set forth in Table XXV.

TABLE XXV

VOCATIONAL EXPERIENCE OF MEMBERS OF TWO RELIGIOUS COMMUNITIES FOR WOMEN

1st Religious Community for Women	2nd Religious Community for Women
146 Teaching Sisters	260 Teaching Sisters (15–20 Teach Music only)
Occupational Experience	*Occupational Experience*
9 Teachers in Public Schools	22 Teachers in Public Schools
25 Secretarial and Office Positions	63 Secretarial and Stenographic
6 Nurses	7 Other Business Positions
1 Mechanical Draftsman	1 Lawyer
1 Designer	4 Artists
1 Artist	3 Teachers of Music
1 Teacher of Music	
44—32%	100—40%

The 1934 census of Catholic high schools shows 13,258 Religious men and women teaching. If even one-third of this number has had business and professional experience, it would seem that an ample number could qualify as vocational counselors at least as far as occupational experience is concerned.

White House Conference Report

Heretofore, the White House Conference Report, Education and Training, Subcommittee on Vocational Guidance, has been the only overview of the status of guidance from a comprehensive viewpoint. In view of the data presented in this study, the investigator feels justified in saying that the data on Catholic secondary schools presented in this Report are not indicative of conditions in Catholic high schools today. Exact comparison cannot be made inasmuch as the basis of the Report was diocesan organization, while the basis of this study was the individual school.

Results of the Questionnaire Distribution

The distribution of the questionnaire to obtain data has served for wide propaganda—a situation that had not been foreseen. Letters were received from many states requesting copies for the school files; 87 requests for specific advice relative to techniques, texts, and courses came to the investigator, and more than one hundred others for smaller services, bibliography, and results of this study. This was a great encouragement, for one of the aims of the questionnaire was to arouse interest. It was hoped, as stated elsewhere, that a background picture of conditions and present practices and attitudes would serve for planning programs and courses in the immediate future to extend the interest and work in vocational and educational guidance, and to ensure that the interest should eventuate in action. In the opinion of the investigator, this hope has been justified. It is time for action.

Summary of Present Status

In Chapter V it has been shown that, beginning with interest in those students who believed themselves called to Religious life, teachers in Catholic high schools extended their interest to those who were choosing secular vocations, ensuring higher education to those students who seemed capable of profiting by it. These efforts for students were personal and unorganized. Inevitably teachers overlooked students just as capable as those cared for, and the need was observed for an organized program to include all students in this personal interest, and to include all phases required for all students.

Studies reviewed in Chapter III had covered Catholic schools in some areas of the United States and schools of particular sizes. A nation-wide survey was deemed necessary and was begun by the writer in 1934, to determine basic conditions preliminary to recommending programs of guidance. All the states and the District of Columbia were represented in the responses, and 85% of the dioceses. These schools responding were typical of all Catholic high schools in the United States in respect to geographical distribution, distribution to various size cities and rural areas, to types of schools, to classification of students, and to size of high schools. The data, therefore, may be termed typical of all Catholic high schools of the United States. Questionnaires had been sent to 1,648 schools with students ranging from 25, the minimum size included, to 2,970. Of these 1,648 schools, 1,004, 61%, responded; students in these high schools were 61% of students in the 1934 census. Eighty-one per cent of the respondents were interested in vocational guidance, and two-thirds of these had become interested through observing the need for guidance; the other one-third through their own reading, addresses, and state or diocesan programs of guidance.

Of schools responding, 49.6% stated that they provided for vocational guidance, and 10.3% more stated that they gave guidance informally, i.e., with program unorganized. One hundred schools indicated that they had begun guidance work in the decades 1910 to 1930, and 159 schools had begun work 1930 to 1934. Guidance had been introduced in the ninth grade in 50% of the high schools, both junior and four-year type. In the beginning, 78% of those reporting on the item used informal guidance; 22% began with the class organized. Home-room teachers were used in beginning guidance in almost one-half of the schools responding. Of the 321 schools reporting on this item, 31% had increased the time devoted to guidance techniques, for reasons specifically stated.

Fourteen guidance techniques were mentioned on the questionnaire. The one most frequently recorded was student interviews with teachers and school officers; addresses by representatives of vocations ranked second, while third place was held by assembly talks of school officers and by referring students to vocational literature; follow-up of graduates ranked fourth, followed by case studies of students' problems and student interviews with representatives of vocations; five or less per cent of schools responding used occupational observation and field-trips, clubs, and follow-up of bright or failing students, or students who had dropped out, physical examinations, and meetings after school when school time was not available. Emphasis seemed to have been placed upon follow-up of the failing rather than the bright students—indicating that training for leadership had been slighted.

In 34% of the schools responding, intelligence tests were used in guidance; in 26%, achievement tests; and in 17%, character study and practice; 9% had used aptitude tests, but the majority expressed themselves as dissatisfied with these as objective evidence for guidance purposes; tests of mechanical ability had been used in 2%, and personnel inventory in 4% of the schools responding.

The class in occupations was maintained in 10% of the schools in the study, and of these, 38 schools—almost 4%—required the work, some granting credit, the average being one-half unit, or one credit. In three schools the work was required, but no credit was granted. Of the 35 schools (3.4%) offering the work as an elective, nine gave no credit, and the majority gave one credit. Most of these courses in occupations, offered for one year, were placed in the ninth grade, but 45% of the schools reporting on this item extended the course over two to four years.

Counselors had interviews relative to occupational plans with students in 29% of the schools responding, and almost half of these interviewed all students. Of the school officers responding to this study 10% had knowledge of federal, state or city surveys; school officers and students with local agencies co-operating had made many such surveys themselves. Less than 4%, however, maintained files of current occupational data, but the condition of industry and commerce must be considered as contributing to this situation. It may have been partly responsible also for the low number—15%—of school officers who indicated that placement work was carried on in their schools, and 13% followed up the students they had placed. Many of the counselors stated that placement and follow-up would be resumed with the improvement of the industrial and commercial situation; that they had carried on such work previously. The use of organized alumni to assist students was noted in only 9% of the schools, but counselors assist alumni to get jobs, scholarships, and provide other services in 37% of the schools responding.

Guidance records were kept by almost 10% of the schools, but only half have them centralized for faculty use. Guidance in education for the choice of technical school or college was reported by 52% of the schools responding.

In the administration of guidance, 45% of the principals acted as counselors; in 22% of the schools, other school officers acted in that capacity; 16% of the schools in the study had counselors, 2.3% being full-time workers; 11% of these counselors had had special training for counseling. Part-time counselors were drawn from many departments of school studies. Of the five titles used, Student Counselor was found most frequently. Training had been secured by the 110 counselors mentioned above, in 21 of the colleges and universities specified. Time devoted to counseling duties by part-time counselors was widely varied.

Members of Religious Communities acted as counselors in 27% of the schools in this study; this per cent included counselors and school officers acting as counselors, while in 10% of the schools the counselor was a priest. A question of the feasibility of Religious men and women acting as counselors arose some years ago—particularly concerning Religious women. It was decided in the affirmative, the evidence presented showing that many of them were amply able to care for the work, to the advantage of the students. The writer sought objective evidence of this feasibility, and found 32% in one Community, and 40% in the other, who had occupational experience and thus could qualify on this point for counseling duties. If even 32% of the 13,258 Religious men and women who are listed in the 1934 census of Catholic high school teachers have had such experience as these two Religious Communities indicate, there should be no fear as to the feasibility of their being counselors.

In view of the facts obtained in this study, the writer felt justified in saying that the evidence of vocational guidance in Catholic high schools presented in the White House Conference Report, Education and Training, Subcommittee on Vocational Guidance is not representative of conditions as they are today, whatever may have been their authenticity in 1930, although only 72 of the 105 dioceses in the United States were covered, and replies quoted from 15 of these.

CHAPTER VI

CONCLUSIONS

CATHOLIC educators are increasingly alert to the student's need for vocational guidance. Evidence to confirm this statement is found in these facts: the attitudes of interest expressed by educators in response to questionnaires and letters to the investigator with questions both specific and general concerning courses, texts, and techniques; the emphasis on vocational guidance in educational conferences, literature, and research; the programs, both tentative and organized, in our high schools; two diocesan programs already set up and functioning; other dioceses urging or requiring inclusion of guidance activities; Catholic high schools co-operating with city or state programs of vocational guidance; the serious attempts of secondary schools, large and small, urban and rural, to include feasible guidance activities in their educational programs. All this activity is an effort to meet a need expressed several years ago by the San Francisco *Monitor:* "Many loyal and patient parents look forward to the day when some local Catholic educational institutions or some lay society will set up agencies for giving vocational advice to our parochial, high, and college students, and young people beginning in the world." This same need was expressed recently by graduates of Catholic colleges who had continued their education in universities and who were asked wherein their college work had "been found wanting" or what desirable elements should have been included. Several of the one hundred questioned stated that vocational guidance was the most important thing which their colleges had failed to give them. [56]

Agencies for Disseminating the Idea

If the need for vocational guidance is recognized by leading Catholic educators, what effort have they made to acquaint the rank and file of teachers with techniques or devices to meet this need? What practical plans have been made by organizations other than schools to give vocational guidance?

A review in Chapter II of the Catholic educational literature shows an increasing emphasis on vocational guidance; for the 1932 and 1933 *Proceedings* of the National Catholic Education Association devoted 20% and 15% respectively to this one topic. We have shown the interest manifested by education conferences of Religious Communities and by students of research in vocational guidance. There has been sufficient publicity for educators to be familiar with guidance practices and principles. The Sodality mentioned in Chapter V has suggested and urged a vocational week in schools when representatives of various vocations should be invited to address the school assemblies and interview students, and thus interest people of the community in the schools. Many school officers initiated the vocational guidance week as a result of this suggestion, expressed repeatedly in *The Queen's Work,* the organ of the Sodality. Knights of Columbus, through their educational program, better known as "Boy Work," and Catholic Big Brothers and Sisters have assisted in disseminating the idea, and have given valuable help and service in many cities. The troops of Boy Scouts, Girl Scouts, Columbian Squires, and Catholic Boys' Brigade have all offered opportunities for spreading the guidance idea and putting it into practice.

Guidance Is the Norm of Catholic Education

The Prologue attempted to show that the "Rule" of St. Benedict, which is the foundation for so many Religious Communities today, is a prototype of modern guidance techniques. The Encyclical letters of Popes have emphasized guidance, and the practice of prominent educators has always included it. Dr. Nicholas Murray Butler, in *The Meaning of Education,* says: "The monastery schools and famous establishments of Saint Gall, Reichenau, and Fulda are the direct ancestors of our Etons and Rugbys, of our contemporary lycées, gymnasia, and academies." [88] The continuity of Catholic education through many centuries has yielded a wealth of experience in guidance of students, for those entering secular vocations as well as those having Religious vocations. The whole practice of the Church has emphasized individualization in the milieu of social life—the dignity and value of each individual soul maintained in every relationship, personal and social.

The Industrial Revolution and succeeding economic and industrial changes blunted the guiding of the youth of Europe, and the rapid settlement and growth of the United States, with its myriad opportunities, postponed the inauguration of guidance here. Today, guidance is imperative, and especially so for Catholic high schools with 92% urban students and 55% of these students in cities with population over 100,000.

Findings in Catholic Secondary Schools

The interest of Catholic educators in vocational guidance has its source in observation of the need for it. This interest has been growing slowly but steadily over a period of twenty-five years, as has been shown (1) in Chapter II in the review of Catholic educational literature; (2) in Chapter III in the review of research which included data on vocational guidance and investigations of the status of guidance in Catholic schools; (3) in Chapter VII which presents facilities for training counselors and teachers with a vocational guidance viewpoint in Catholic colleges and universities.

This question intrudes itself insistently: if there has been such interest in guidance expressed in educational literature, why has practice lagged so far behind? The investigator considers from evidence at hand that many factors contribute toward that condition in Catholic schools which are paralleled in public schools. Vocational guidance is often confused with vocational training, which is the training for skills, and requires expensive equipment, specially trained, skilled teachers, and additional space and time in school. The economic situation has necessitated the curtailing of expense, and inclusion of only immediate necessities in Catholic schools. The teaching loads of Catholic teachers have demanded their complete attention, in and out of school hours, so that few could be relieved for guidance purposes. Growth of guidance services has been retarded also by lack of funds, and lack of trained personnel. Resources for Catholic schools must come from people who have paid taxes to support public schools and who pay additionally to support Catholic schools. Each item added to the educational program means a corresponding financial burden. Therefore it has been necessary for Catholic educators to probe deep into educational plans, and to be severe in evaluation before making additions to curricula and staff.

Provision for vocational guidance for students was reported by 50% of the schools responding to the questionnaire, and informal guidance was reported by an additional 10%. Since schools responding are located in all the states and the District of Columbia, and since the distribution of respondents as to geographical areas, various sized cities and rural territory, type of high schools, size of schools, and classification of student bodies, is representative of all Catholic high schools, the conditions disclosed may be said to be representative of all Catholic secondary schools. It is true that much of the guidance provided does not reach all students, lacks clear-cut objectives, and inclusion of all phases which are desirable and necessary for aiding students. The investigator considers this slower, but solid growth infinitely preferable to mushroom growth which might have collapsed. It is true that school officers have had, in some cases, vague ideas of just what constitutes a guidance program, but even specialists in the guidance field are at opposite poles in their recommendations and in techniques. Catholic educators have considered it wise to proceed slowly.

Providing vocational guidance necessitates the presentation of occupational information, since choosing a vocation presupposes a knowledge of vocations sufficient to constitute a choice. Knowledge is necessary for the deliberate choice of either a religious or a secular vocation, and deliberate choice is the only solid foundation. The investigator considers that this phase of guidance—occupational information—is the weakest point in the vocational guidance in Catholic secondary schools. This choice of vocational objective must assist in the choice of courses and subjects, the choice of higher technical schools or colleges—which are included in educational guidance in both high school and college.

Addresses by representatives of professions and business men and by teachers and other school officers have been the means most frequently used for disseminating vocational information. This is a good beginning, but it is only a beginning, and too many schools have stopped there on the threshold. When occupational interest has been initiated, it should be developed by analysis of the occupation by the student, and analysis of himself to determine his ability to meet the requirements of the work. Vocational civics, English themes on the subject, occupational correlation with school subjects in regular classes, and referring students to vocational literature were some of the devices employed—in addition to the class in occupations, or the class in guidance—to disseminate occupational information. There was little uniformity in the location of the class in occupations reported by the schools. Follow-up of graduates will usually indicate trends and emphases on certain occupations important for that individual school.

Clubs, occupational field trips, and meetings after school (when an opportunity is not presented during school hours) were not used for guidance in the degree which the investigator expected to find. The use of physical examination to confirm or deter vocational choice seems to be overlooked, and very few have realized the value of discussing case studies of students' problems. Co-ordination of schools and community agencies relative to current employment data seems almost a minus quantity, yet current data are essential to placement; they constitute the functioning point of vocational guidance. The value of placing books on guidance in the school library has not been considered sufficiently. In the use of tests, Catholic schools have made a beginning, but aptitude and prognostic tests and personality rating sheets are not widely known. Aptitude tests have not been developed to a satisfactory point, which fact may account for their neglect by these schools.

Individual counseling, which has always been a technique in Catholic schools, and group counseling, which has grown up with vocational guidance, both seem to have received a new impetus. The inclusion of all students in the individual counseling plans of Catholic high schools seems to the investigator a very hopeful sign. Follow-up of failing students to reduce failures, inferiority complexes, and consequent loss of time is most necessary in counseling, but the problems of failing students must not be given preference, as responses seem to show they are. The stimulating of gifted children and the urging of normal students to maintain their capacity are the proper points of emphasis. The developing of necessary leadership is the reason for guidance of superior and normal students. The gifted should be visioned as our leaders, and should therefore be the objects of the greatest expenditure of energy on the part of the teachers.

Educational Guidance

Educational guidance as stated on the questionnaire related merely to the choice of college or technical school. While 52% of the schools gave this guidance, it served only the students continuing their education in schools. As stated in Chapter IV 53% of students in 1928 continued their education in college or technical school, but that this percentage was reduced to 43% in 1932 because of the economic situation. Whether or not every effort was made to secure scholarships for gifted students not able to continue education was not asked, but from a knowledge of practices in Catholic high schools, the investigator believes every effort was made to secure them. College preparatory schools need to give guidance, but have not yet realized the fact. Many take the stand expressed by one school, "All our students go on to college, so vocational guidance is not necessary for our pupils." Evidently school officers do not realize that secondary school age is the point at which tentative choice should be made, at least, of occupation, with consequent choice of college, of course, and of subjects. The assuming of responsibility in making a decision as to possible occupation is the point of departure from youth to adulthood. The habit of making such decisions must be cultivated to prevent drifting in life, but school officers without such vision will not assist students to reach their maximum stature of character and mind.

Placement, Follow-up, and Records

Placement and follow-up, two important phases of guidance, have decreased because of general business conditions—according to respondents' statements—and because of increased duties on the part of school officers. Respondents indicated willingness to resume these very important functions, but a greater knowledge and understanding of labor conditions seem necessary. Placement seems the culmination of guidance activities preceding it, so that the investigator had expected a much larger return from high schools—at least in the experimental stage. The reason for this situation is not apparent. Was it lack of time? Was it fear that the schools were burdening themselves with a function which properly did not belong to them, in their estimation? Was it absorption in academic education? Or was it lack of visioning man as a whole, educating all his powers?

The status of student cumulative records for guidance purposes was not at all satisfactory. As has been said before, Catholic educators are required to do so much that they frequently must make choice between doing the work, and recording it. The importance of these records for continuity of guidance and for optimal means of assisting the individual student has not been understood, in the opinion of the investigator. If a choice of work must be made, counseling must take precedence of records, for assistance to the individual is the aim of guidance. But assistance will be so variant without a cumulative record that it will cease to be an aid, and become a hindrance to the student.

Administration of Guidance

In organization of guidance, no one alone of the program practices outlined in the summary of Chapter V is typical of Catholic secondary schools, for all are in use. The investigator doubts that any one type should be considered for adoption, or could serve the varied needs of dioceses with such widely divergent interests. In the smaller schools guidance is carried on through regular administrative officers, through home-room advisers, both trained and untrained, and, in some instances, through counselors. Since they have larger faculties, the high schools of middle size, with 200 to 500 students, and the large schools with enrollments ranging from 500 to 3,000 students, have made greater effort to organize the work of guidance so that all students may profit by it, although administrative officers functioned as counselors in a large per cent of these schools also. In number, more counselors were found in the smaller high schools, but comparatively, these schools showed a lower percentage than the large-size schools. Sister M. Priscilla's study, reviewed in Chapter III, declared there was a high positive correlation between the size of the high school surveyed, and the extent of the guidance activities and the presence of a counselor. When percentages were compared in the present study, we may say that this positive correlation was well defined.

Counselors and home-room teachers seemed to determine the scope of the guidance activities, sometimes with very little encouragement either from administrative officers or from other faculty members. Only their interest in the individual student, and their belief that guidance work will be general before long, induced them to maintain the work. It seems, in summing the reports presented, that the individual faculty member who is interested in guidance is the key to progress in vocational guidance. Where there is real interest, that person cannot be hindered, guidance will break through in an organized form, and continue as long as that interested person is on the faculty, and this activity will be repeated in whatever school that person teaches.

Data indicated that principals acted as counselors in almost one-half of the schools responding, and other school officers in about one-fourth of the schools. Counselors were found in 15.4% of the schools; 10.9% of these counselors had had training in various colleges and universities; one-seventh were full-time counselors, and Religious formed almost one-half of those who served as counselors—principals, other school officers, and counselors. Many persons serving as counselors evidently had not realized how much they might gain from training, and from urging faculty to adopt a guidance viewpoint. They had not realized what great benefits their students would derive from their training for vocational guidance. Teaching is a foundation for counseling, but the counselor's is a profession separate from teaching, going on beyond teaching, and requiring the mastery of techniques other than the techniques of teaching.

A beginning has been made, and much preparatory work has been done. "Neglect and lack of enthusiasm" one questionnaire stated as the reason for not allowing more time for guidance; this is a frank statement of a fault, but the recognition of causes usually precedes constructive changes. Catholic high schools are educating more than a quarter of a million students, and must give attention to their vocational guidance. Prominent Catholic educators, public school officials, social workers, judges, and legislators are urging increased attention to vocational guidance. Catholic secondary school students should have the advantages of co-operation with community plans, and the collaboration of all agencies which make possible effective vocational and educational guidance. Such guidance is consonant with both the principles and the standard practice in Catholic education. Catholic Religious teachers, who have generously given their lives to the education of America's youth, will not shrink from this added burden. Pope Pius XI wrote in his Encyclical on Christian Education, "Perfect schools are the result not so much of good methods as of good teachers, teachers who are thoroughly prepared and well-grounded in the matter they have to teach; who possess the intellectual and moral qualifications required by their important office; who cherish a pure and holy love for the youths confided to them; and who have therefore sincerely at heart the true good of family and country." It is through the individualizing educational and vocational guidance that they shall accomplish the education which "takes in the whole aggregate of human life, not with a view of reducing it in any way, but in order to elevate, regulate and perfect it, in accordance with the example and teaching of Christ."

CHAPTER VII

FACILITIES FOR TRAINING COUNSELORS UNDER
CATHOLIC AUSPICES

Statistics of Catholic Universities and Colleges

THE Catholic Directory of Schools and Colleges, 1932-1933, was the latest printed list of Catholic Universities and Colleges. Pages 29 to 108 revealed 162 universities and colleges, and 44 normal training schools for Religious. Of these 162, 26 were universities and 136 were colleges. Eighteen of the 26 universities listed courses in Education, eight did not. Of the 136 colleges, 70 listed courses in Education, 66 did not.

Survey of Colleges and Universities Having Courses in Education

Questionnaires were forwarded to all universities and colleges which listed any of the following among their offerings: Education, Teacher Training, Extension Courses, Teachers' Certificate Courses, Teachers' Summer Courses. Four questions were asked:

1) Does your college offer courses in Educational and Vocational Guidance in preparation of counselors, or teachers for secondary schools? Yes — No —.
2) If yes, will you indicate these courses by name, whether graduate or undergraduate, and forward catalog or bulletin.
3) Are any of these courses required either for the baccalaureate or graduate degrees? Yes — No —.
4) Is Vocational and Educational Guidance included in courses for school administrators? Yes — No —.

These questionnaires were sent in December 1934 to all 18 universities having education courses, and to 47 of the 70 colleges. Elimination of the 23 colleges was made either because of their being corporate colleges of universities sent questionnaires—since it was known that the same policies obtain in these cases—or because of the small size of the student body.

Return from Questionnaire

A 100% return was secured by a postcard reminder sent to a very few colleges. These universities and colleges are located in the District of Columbia and in twenty-four states, not localized, but scattered over the United States.

One university had given up its education course in favor of the Diocesan Teachers' College in the same city which offers a full roster of standard courses. One college prepares only the elementary teachers.

One university and nine colleges replied in the negative regarding guidance courses, although one college stated that a member of the faculty was seeking training which would enable him to return and give courses in vocational guidance; another college felt that students would gain some knowledge from the guidance techniques then in use at the college. One university and four colleges which had not previously offered guidance courses stated that instructors and courses were in preparation, to be begun, one in February, the others in September 1935. These plans have been fulfilled.

Of the remaining 55 universities and colleges, 28 offer courses in vocational guidance, ranging from one course to many, covering all phases, including clinical experience and field work. One college presents the work only to the sisters and school administrators of its own Community; one university presents guidance courses only in summer; 25 offer guidance phases and techniques in other courses, having 21 titles such as: Secondary Education, Secondary School Administration, Psychology of Adolescence, Junior High Schools, and Character Education. These courses are listed under various departments: Education, Psychology, Religion, Philosophy, and in some cases students may receive credit in either of two departments; some are undergraduate, some graduate, some courses may be either. Only one college requires guidance courses for a degree—a graduate degree; a few colleges require such courses of those majoring in secondary education, but these requirements are found in states known to be supporting and encouraging guidance work. One college which offers pre-theological work urges students entering theology to take the guidance courses. The influence of this may be gauged from the fact that they will work with parochial schools as principals or supervising pastors.

TABLE XXVI

CATHOLIC UNIVERSITIES AND COLLEGES OFFERING EXTENDED WORK IN GUIDANCE

(*Religious community sponsoring the college is indicated in parentheses*)

California	Immaculate Heart College, Hollywood (I.H.M.)
District of Columbia	*Catholic University of America (Hierarchy)
Illinois	*Loyola University, Chicago, (S.J.)
Indiana	*University of Notre Dame (C.S.C.)
Louisiana	Loyola University of the South, New Orleans, (S.J.)
Michigan	*Marygrove College, Detroit, (I.H.M.) (to own Sisters only)
Minnesota	College of St. Catherine, St. Paul, Minn., (S.S.J.)
Missouri	*St. Louis University, (S.J.)
Nebraska	Creighton University, Omaha, (S.J.)
New York	*Fordham University, New York City, (S.J.)
Ohio	*John Carroll University, Cleveland, (S.J.)
	Toledo Teachers' College—Diocesan
Pennsylvania	*Immaculata College, Immaculata, Pa., (I.H.M.)
	*Marywood College, Scranton, (I.H.M.)
Washington	*Gonzaga University, Spokane, (S.J.)
Wisconsin	*Marquette University, Milwaukee, (S.J.)

* Indicates special alertness to Guidance Work.

TABLE XXVII

SUMMARY OF OFFERINGS IN GUIDANCE IN CATHOLIC COLLEGES AND
UNIVERSITIES

	All	Offer Education Courses	Offer Many Courses in Guidance	Present Guidance in High School Administration Courses	Present Guidance in Other Courses
Number of Universities	26	18	8	4	7
Number of Colleges...	136	70	16	15	32
Total..........	162	88	24	19	39

Summary

Every section of the United States is represented in Table XXVI, listing 16 colleges and universities in 14 states and the District of Columbia, which offer many courses in vocational guidance.

Altogether, 28 colleges and universities offer these courses, and one additional college uses guidance techniques with its own students; six others were looking forward to adding guidance courses in the immediate future. Two other colleges, which do not have guidance courses, have attempted to make students guidance-conscious, the one by a required paper on guidance with bibliography, the other by a prize contest each year for a contribution on guidance. The latter aims not at original research, but at acquainting students with literature on the subject, functions and phases, and their history. One college requires guidance courses for a graduate degree; a few colleges require such courses of those who are majoring in secondary education. Table XXVII gives a summary of the offerings in guidance in the Catholic colleges and universities.

There is opportunity, under Catholic auspices, to secure training in vocational guidance. Students in courses must be impressed with the need for this work, and with a desire to continue study and research in the field. Those who have completed courses should be urged to make concrete plans suitable for conditions in individual schools, and then see them through to a practical success.

CHAPTER VIII

RECOMMENDATIONS

THE FACT that two-thirds of the respondents in this study indicated their interest in vocational and educational guidance, and also indicated that their interest was solidly based on personal observation of the students' need for guidance, demonstrated to the investigator that the ground had been prepared for introducing guidance into Catholic secondary schools, and data returned showed that a beginning had been made.

It is assumed that educators are desirous of turning interest into effective activity, and are searching for ways and means. This assumption is confirmed by the many requests for assistance accompanying questionnaires returned.

The work has been retarded by three things, according to reports received: (1) Confusion of vocational guidance with vocational training, (2) consequent fear of heavy expense in introducing the work because of lack of funds, and (3) lack of counselors and teachers trained in guidance. If many teachers and counselors are given training in colleges and universities offering the work, the first two hindrances to vocational guidance will disappear. This is the first recommendation for making interest concrete: Train teachers and counselors. This leads to the second recommendation, that more colleges offer extensive courses in vocational guidance.

The objective of the counselor must be twofold: first, providing the student with opportunity to analyze himself, his achievements, abilities, and capacities; and second, teaching to the student sources of occupational information and matters which he must consider, with evaluation and interpretation of such occupational information. The training of the counselor, therefore, must include preparation for this twofold objective.

The teacher who is chosen for training as counselor should be selected for his human interest and love of personnel work, and his ability to contribute much to the lives of students, and to impart knowledge in an interesting and stimulating way. This presupposes knowledge of psychology—particularly adolescent and experimental psychology—sociology, and labor conditions and problems, although the last two named may be secured during training for counselor's duties.

In training, emphasis should be placed upon fundamental principles and practices of vocational and educational guidance, occupational information and its sources—and therefore library facilities—together with possible methods for presenting occupational information. The analysis of occupations is important, as is also the objective means for knowing students. These tests and rating scales, so far as they are practicable today in shedding partial light on students' abilities and achievements, should be handled easily by trained counselors, and, in this accepted phase of training, emphasis should be on interpretation of tests and scales. The value and forms of records should be grasped in order to insure continuity of guidance. Understanding types of interviews, and the diplomacy required for securing information from students, with consequent responsibility for sacredly guarding confidences, must be the preparation for individual counseling, the most important phase of the guidance program. The counselor's knowledge of the student's home and personal background is a phase, the value of which must be emphasized in training. The making of case studies, and interpretation of their essential features, is another technique to be learned in training.

Great emphasis should be placed upon the possibilities of developing much-needed leadership through guidance of the bright. They should receive greater attention than students of lesser abilities or those who are failing, since the bright have capacities fitting them to assume leadership. This should in nowise be construed to minimize reasonable attention due to students who may be failing because of faulty preparation. In many instances, the personal interest of the counselor is sufficient motivating force to raise an average student into the leadership group.

A survey of the students in the counselor's individual school will determine many techniques. Resident schools and schools drawing students from various localities will require the presentation of all occupations, and such guidance that students may determine their own cities' occupational potentialities. Schools drawing students from the schools' immediate locality may need only local occupational information, but review of alumni will usually assist in deciding whether all occupations should be emphasized, or only local occupations. Contacts possible in the counselor's home city and specific employment opportunities there constitute phases of self-activity for the counselor to investigate during training and after it. Information in regard to agencies which are interested in vocational guidance, and which will co-operate with counselors will be gained during training, then discovered and visited by the counselor in his home city.

The investigator appreciates and endorses the attitude that the choice of lifework is a momentous matter for both the individual and for society, for time and for eternity. This attitude demonstrates an understanding of abilities and capacities as gifts of God, to be developed by us, and of the fact that we must render an account at death of the development and proper use of our talents—so far as this has been possible. These are Catholic principles.

Two fallacies are present in Catholic schools, relative to vocational guidance: first, that all guidance is being taken care of in Religion classes, and second, that priests by virtue of their college and seminary training are fully equipped to render guidance for any and all occupational fields. The writer knows from experience the need for assisting students in Religion classes—during this adolescent age—to arrive at a philosophy of life which shall serve for the entire lifetime. Insofar as lifework enters into that philosophy of life, it must be considered in the Religion class; but there is such a body of specific matter in religion and in the occupational field that no one class can embody all of both. A smattering of either one is unsatisfactory. Priests, from their preparatory work and social experience, have the background for effective vocational guidance, and have in addition—in many cases—the specific data necessary for religious vocations. But specific data for other vocations must be acquired by them if they are to advise students relative to all vocations and occupations. If, as in the case of St. Ambrose College, Davenport, Iowa, prospective priests take the course in vocational and educational guidance as a part of the preparation for their educational supervision in parish schools, this condition will disappear in the course of time. This college and any others doing the same effective work cannot be too highly commended.

Guidance for the handicapped and for children in orphanages and other institutions requires the training of the counselor with relation to his particular problem, which will involve a specialized psychology, and a knowledge of research studies and experience in the particular field and of specialized occupations suitable for these children. An extended medical knowledge, child psychology, and sociology are necessary also. Mental hygiene must function more vitally with these pupils than with students of normal life.

Table V shows an increase of students in Catholic secondary schools in rural areas; while the number of schools decreased about 7%, from 1930 to 1932, the number of students increased 15%. This seems to indicate a consolidation of schools with increased average enrollment. Vocational guidance activities therefore become more necessary in these schools to assist the individual pupil. Rural students coming to high school usually show a variety of achievement, and home and school training wider than in urban localities. Carefully planned and confidential autobiographies of students will reveal personal problems and attitudes which call for a maximum of guidance. The first step will be to gain the student's confidence, for many will not know that they have problems, or will not be able to analyze their difficulties. Family and personal background will be very important, and should be discovered from sources in addition to the biography. As a rule, students know little about opportunities, either educational or vocational, outside the locality. An understanding must be gained of these opportunities, yet with sane, common-sense viewpoint, lest "far fields seem greener." Many students know only house and farm work, but wish the more refined arts and handicrafts. People from small towns, and farmers have too long been held up to ridicule and laughter on the page, the stage, and the screen. The dignity of work, its contribution, and the almost infinite worth of man must be impressed upon students. In general, no effort should be made to urge students either to stay in rural areas or to leave them. A view of the rural world through the eyes of economists, of agricultural specialists, and of successful merchants and farmers will assist all students. Imagination can be developed in a healthful and helpful way through literature, art, and current periodicals.

Studies made on rural youths reveal that they like things they have learned to do, and are conditioned toward many interesting activities unknown to them. This is a very human trait, and the attitude offers almost infinite possibilities for the counselor. Because of the simple life in rural sections, the small social groups, and the regular duties with little actual money for work, urban life wears a rosy glow to the average student from rural areas. Enriching the life of students with understanding of actual conditions, with understanding of many occupations and their requirements, with social, artistic, and literary activities for self-development and confidence, will be the most valuable contribution within the power of the counselor. The student in these rural areas, will, as a rule, receive less assistance from parents and will therefore depend more on the teacher's guidance. Enriching the student's life will result in enriching the home in which the student lives. The world of books, periodicals, and reading can be made attractive and observation may be stimulated, so that a desire for study and education will result. Tact must be exercised in helping rural students to gain a knowledge of self, for they, as a rule, are more sensitive than boys and girls in cities who have many varied interests. On the other hand, rural students will usually have attained a variety of skills, with a more normal outlook on life and more self-dependence, than students in the artificial atmosphere of a large city.

With less of distraction and more of responsibility within a limited circle of experiences, the student in rural areas will have had to work out for himself a fundamental understanding of the interplay of nature with man, but will lack much of the social understanding of those who live in more populous areas. This social understanding, by its very absence, may become an objective of the student, and here guidance becomes extremely valuable in interpreting a balance between the values of social life and "the solitude of creative work." Social conventions, to the student in rural areas, are at once a desire and a despair in many instances. An interpretation of these, with a supplying of books and pamphlets of worth, will do much in developing self-confidence.

A study of actual occupations in the locality will broaden the student's views and make a specific foundation for knowledge of all occupations. Capable students should receive careful and personal guidance for further education. The question of books on occupations for the library may be solved by borrowing from the county or the state library. These books may be returned, and others secured, so that a desirable list may be reviewed in a year. Well-prepared lessons may result in a reward of a reading period at an improvised library table, if space is lacking for a library. Themes on occupations offer a new motivation and a splendid opportunity for discussion and oral themes —usually needed to develop opinions—and speech training. Leadership is developed in oral themes, in club work, and class-club work, and self-consciousness is lost in this interesting subject. Students interested in the same occupation may form committees to investigate and report to the class, so that all may have the value of the committee's work. In this case desirable phases of information should be suggested by the teacher as assistance to the committee in beginning work; an outline should be prepared by the students for visé by the teacher, before preparation of the report may be completed or before the report is given to the student body. Speakers may be invited to address groups interested, interviews may be arranged with persons engaged in the occupation, radio talks may be utilized as well as exhibits and visual aids, such as films or pictures. Any means of securing correct information should be put into service.

Study of the personality of each pupil and use of psychological tests should accompany the instruction and counseling given to each pupil. Means for tryout experience should be supplied wherever possible. If placement is possible the student best fitted for the particular position should be recommended, and information should be given to the student selected, relative to what is expected of him, desirable traits, some problems he will encounter in human relationships, and principles of conduct which will apply in that case. Follow-up should keep the teacher or counselor in touch with the one employed, resolving any difficulties, if possible, and interpreting any puzzling situations. Much personal and health guidance, and stimulation to reading and further study may be necessary for advancement in work, or for an incentive to further education. If higher education is possible, the counselor should assist, as in other schools, with choice of a college or school whose work is standard, and should arouse the interest of persons who may assist capable students with scholarships or funds.

In planning for administration of guidance, the county will serve as a convenient unit (but individual schools need not wait for a county organization before beginning work). A similarity of problems and a community of interests will bind faculty and students in such a division. Professional reading may well follow this guidance work, with benefit to teachers and students. If no other counselor is available, the principal may serve until some teacher who is interested in the work has read widely on the subject and taken courses, where possible. This teacher may function as an understudy to the principal in teaching occupations and conducting interviews. Where the work is undertaken as a county unit, the director of guidance or counselor will direct and co-ordinate efforts, stimulating, advising, instructing. There is no set plan or program of guidance, but the need and the convenience of all concerned should be the criteria, in that particular environment.

Provision for Vocational Guidance

Providing for vocational guidance may assume many forms, informal as well as organized. If organization must be delayed for one reason or another, informal guidance may be begun in English classes through theme work; in all subject-matter classes, where the bearing of subject matter on various occupations is shown; in Religion classes where a stimulus is given to survey occupations and study self, since the need for this has been recognized and provided for in modern texts on Religion. A unit on lifework is included in these modern texts, with suggestions for development. Extracurricular activities may be utilized also for occupational information and serve, in a manner, for a tryout of particular abilities. Meetings after school for guidance work are sometimes resorted to until arrangements can be made to use school time. In all cases, adjustable plans should be made, and introduced tentatively to determine their feasibility. If organization is possible, it may take the form of a class in Guidance, Vocational Civics, Occupations class with the home room organized for guidance, and individual counseling of students. Faculty and students should be gradually initiated, or there is developed a resistance instead of assistance and co-operation.

Occupational Information

Since a knowledge of the fields of work, opening of new opportunities, and possible decline and change in others, is a preliminary to choosing an occupation, occupational information is of primary importance to secondary school students. Drifting into crowded fields is an easy matter, either because students do not know other fields, or because they do not realize that the fields are crowded. Many bright students are too modest in the opinion of their abilities, and choose fields below their capacity and achievement, with consequent dissatisfaction, since the use of one's talents to the point of satisfaction is most necessary for personal happiness. But many, many more in the lower levels of ability choose for themselves occupations far above their capacities. Others are urged into them by parents and relatives with the hope of raising the family's social status.

It is a crime against society as well as against the individual to insist upon a child's entering a field where he will not be able to compete with others, will do only mediocre work or possibly fail, and will find no satisfaction. The child is a separate entity, entitled to direct his life into chosen work, within reasonable limits. No real counselor or teacher will decide any student's vocation, nor should parents claim that right, but both teacher and parents should stand by to assist a student to choose, enter upon, and progress in a suitable occupation. Let him explore the fields of interest consonant with his ability and enter upon work with the urge to rise to the top, as far as he is able. In that way lies honor, satisfaction, and a happy life. Our sociology must make students see the interlocking dependence of all occupations, and the fact that sincere and capable work in all fields is everywhere recognized. The world is looking for men to promote in all lines of work, if they will prepare themselves solidly, and then keep on studying and growing after entering upon work. Sterling character is hammered out in such a program of life. These and related ideas and ideals of work and of character must accompany the exploration of fields of occupation. The Encyclical Letter of Pope Leo XIII on "The Condition of Labor" and Pope Pius XI's review of these pronouncements in "The Reconstruction of Society" serve as norms for ideas of economics, labor problems, and sociology which Catholic high schools must impart.

Attitudes and habits of students, developing industry and effective methods of attacking problems can and should be the objective of the teacher, but the matter of the fields of occupation should be the frame on which the attitudes and habits are woven. The concomitants are many. It may be argued that many occupational changes are being made while we are collecting data on occupations. It is true. With the rapid changes in society and in occupations, we cannot expect to give students information which will serve for a lifetime. What we can do is to teach techniques of investigation, sources of information, methods of evaluation, and factors to be considered. These will serve for all time, for guidance is a continuous process and effective self-guidance is the end and aim of guidance. Unless self-activity is developed in the student, all efforts of the teacher are wasted. The student must make tentative choices, explore them, and not expect the counselor to decide, but make his own decisions. He should learn the bearing of all high school subjects upon his selected or tentative field. He should learn also of colleges offering outstanding work in that field, go over catalogs, and discover requirements for admission, with the counselor's assistance. Waste in the educational process will be eliminated by this method, and foresight will be suggested to the student as a desirable habit.

A teacher of occupations must decide for the best interests of her students, whether a survey of all occupations should be given with intensive study of preferred fields, or whether local occupations and employment opportunities should be emphasized. To the writer it seems wise to include all occupations—even though means are not at hand to give complete data; investigations show that all students will not remain in the home locality throughout life. Certainly all occupations should be included in classes in large cities and in smaller places which have easy access to large cities. An acquaintance with possible fields of work established in this manner may bear fruit for the pupil later in life. A check on alumni or alumnae for the preceding ten years will usually demonstrate the needed emphasis—whether on local or on all occupations. Library work is a most important part of teaching occupations, for the knowledge of sources and methods of investigation is intended to function throughout the student's life, making the guidance process continuous.

To arouse interest in the mind of the student relative to his future, so that he may not drift; to acquaint him with practically all fields of work, and their requirements and conditions of work; to teach him sources of information, and how to evaluate them; to indicate matters which should be taken into consideration—physical, intellectual, moral, social, and emotional—as necessary or as desirable; to assist him to study himself, learning to know his own strengths and weaknesses, his talents, comparative abilities, achievements, and skills and the physical, mental, and emotional conditions which must enter into consideration; to urge him to live up to his capacities; to urge him to make use of all educational opportunities possible to him in order to meet competition now and later in life; to teach him, if college or technical school are not possible for him, how he may assist himself to secure a liberal education in other ways; to convince him of the necessity for reading, both vocational and avocational, for study and growth after entering upon work; to inform him of employment procedures and details of interviews which condition favorable or unfavorable attitudes toward applicants; to outline a few plans of business organization, and interrelationships of departments so that the applicant may not be overwhelmed by a strange field—these are the subject matter of the class in guidance and occupations, in addition to the sociological background suggested above.

The suggestion has already been made that themes in English classes may be made the means of expressing interest in vocation, if school officers cannot or do not see the opportunity for introducing a program of guidance. Career books, either of the student's personal design or in printed books, will assist in directing attention to many occupations and sources of information. It seems to the writer that the beginning guidance work should be extensive, and later work intensive, emphasizing occupations of interest to the students. Personal interviews with workers in the chosen field may be arranged through alumni or by the student himself. Biographies also assist the student in understanding the work, the requirements, and the problems of a chosen occupation. Observation of workers by means of field trips helps students to get the atmosphere and spirit of employment. Discussion of case studies by the students will aid them in clear and concrete thinking. Clubs permit tryouts for many fields, but most of all, they permit training for social adjustments, and for understanding the opinions of others.

Personal counseling should supplement group guidance, and should supply specific matter of interest to the student counseled, resolving all difficulties so far as lies in the power of the counselor and stimulating self-activity. Vocational literature in the library of the school and of the city should be used freely to arouse and stimulate interest in the idea of a vocation or an occupation.

Other Aims

Mention has been made in the foregoing section of the guidance of gifted students to make leaders of those with capabilities for leadership. Personal interest of the counselor in average students may raise many into the leaders' group. Failing students should likewise receive aid to bridge difficulties which those particular students are capable of bridging; adjustment of curricula, courses or classes may be required to meet the needs of the failing student and prevent the habit of failure; students who are about to drop out, or promising students who have dropped out, should be followed up, and if possible, returned to school. Interesting prominent persons in these students, and providing scholarships are some means of returning such young people to school. Mention has also been made of physical examination to safeguard the student in his choice of vocation or occupation, and this detail cannot be too deeply impressed on counselors and teachers.

In guidance, student records are to the adviser what case histories and X-ray and laboratory tests are to diagnosticians in the medical field—an absolute necessity. Cumulative records of the American Council on Education may be utilized, or individual school records may be devised—but must be kept current. One means of accomplishing this is the use of students in commercial courses, thus giving practical experience to them, or the use of alumni, or the addition of clerical workers to the principal's or counselor's office until the forms are filled out. Personal items should be entered by the counselor, the principal, or the principal's secretary.

Placement of students in positions, and follow-up are two other recognized phases of guidance. Placement will call for co-operation with the agencies of the city or the community for occupational knowledge and employment possibilities. This requires current data, and for this some provision must be made in the counselor's office. The making of occupational studies is another important duty. Alumni organizations can assist in all this work, and in advising the counselor on various conditions which it is advantageous for him to know. Preparing students for employment interviews is a most important phase of guidance, and demands many of the concomitants of vocational guidance, which will be ineffective without them—personal, social, moral, and adjustive. Talents, skills, and great achievements and capacities are useless without the myriad concomitants which must be discerned and included in plans for educating youth. Alumni should be made to feel that the school has not lost its interest in them upon their graduation, but will supply suggestions, advice, and any co-ordinated action necessary to assist them, which they alone cannot achieve. One of the most effective phases of guidance is the assistance rendered in choosing a college or technical school suited to the interests and objectives of the student. Standards of work should be evaluated and understood by the counselor, not only in the general standard of the college but in specific fields of subject matter, and from the records of students in these subjects following graduation from that college.

Administration of Guidance

The summary of Chapter V has mentioned four types of organization for guidance work, and a fifth may be set up by combination of any or all of these four. Factors determining the type of organization selected may be the community in which the school is located, conditions in the school itself, the student body, and the interest of the faculty or the school public. The writer is firmly convinced that the student body of most high schools can do more to assist in organizing than has been generally realized. Interest aroused, suggestions thrown out, reactions considered, suggestions received, ways and means discussed and then presented to the school public through students—these will dissolve much of the resistance which would be met with otherwise. Then too, students like to see their plans through, so a pride can be aroused, with ample opportunity for adjustment by discussions and suggestions.

When the principal must act as counselor, this counseling function is separated from his administrative functions, and should be so maintained. Under these circumstances, teachers capable of guidance work must become imbued with the idea, should make themselves familiar with techniques and plans for guidance, and should be trained and used in co-operative plans so that the principal will not be working alone, for he can do little or nothing alone. When the principal alone must work out a program of guidance or counseling and related duties, his administrative duties will doubtless hinder the guidance activities.

Specially trained teachers are a hope for smaller schools. With their assistance and advice, plans can be made for disseminating guidance through all the classes and home rooms. The need is for the trained teacher to carry back the ideas to the entire faculty, help to plan with them activities possible in each class, serve as adviser and consultor until all is running smoothly, and be a stimulus always. In addition he must co-operate with city agencies for up-to-date knowledge of conditions, and for the benefit of students in placement and follow-up work. Unless home-room teachers are interested, instructed, advised, and supported by someone with a love for the work and with ability to inspire and direct it, home-room plans of guidance are no more effective than vocational guidance under the principal as the counselor. A time must be set aside when teachers in home rooms are not instructors, but advisers, learning to know students and their needs. It will take time, effort, and practice to accomplish plans, but the results will warrant all.

In the larger schools, adequate provision must be made for vocational guidance. The number of students in such schools precludes individual attention unless some guidance plan is set up, so that the individual student is guided and spurred to maximum achievement. Tables in Chapter IV show many schools with students numbering from 200 to 3,000. A counselor or director of vocational guidance is needed to supply occupational information, make studies, co-ordinate efforts of teachers with administrators on behalf of students, serving for guidance and stimulus. Not all teachers in large high schools can be entrusted with the guidance function, as Chapter V stated, for guidance calls for specific personal qualities and attitudes. Lightening the teaching load of teachers already familiar with the school and with the techniques of teaching is the most effective way of beginning. Training of the counselor is most fruitful and eliminates almost entirely the trial and error method. After planning with school officials, ways and means should be arranged for including all teachers, class sponsors, and special teachers both in discussion and formation of plans, and in carrying out the program.

The counselor will be called upon to help each subject teacher outline the vocational implications of her subject matter. Securing of co-operation is of the utmost necessity. Plans must be made elastic, for no two classes in the same school will be alike in interests, abilities, achievements, tastes, or spirit. Knowing the personality of the class is important for adjusting devices to meet the needs. Slow, steady growth is advisable. The students themselves often can suggest desirable adjustments, if the matter is presented to classes, clubs, or student councils. They have a pride in testing out their suggestions and helping to work them out successfully. One need never fear too many minds focused on vocational guidance plans and adjustments, both of students and of faculty, but the counselor and principal must make final decisions and maintain control since they are directly responsible to school authorities.

Various schools have adopted a period for guidance class suited to their needs. Some use a fifteen-minute period each day, others concentrate all work in a forty-five-minute period each week, and still others use the home-room period each day, with the home-room teachers carrying out the projects planned with the counselor. A complete program of home-room guidance plans may be worked out tentatively for the entire year, and adjustments made as required. The bulletin board, with posters developed by the art department, with newspaper clippings, and with suggestions of interesting articles and books, will do much to keep the current phases before students' minds. If few books are possible for the school library, arrangements may be made with the city, county, or state library for receiving books to be retained a specified time, then replaced by others, until the desired books have all been supplied to students. A school publication also may assist by good, timely articles on guidance phases selected in competition in an English class. Faculty advisers for such school publications should consult with the director or counselor relative to such matters, thus ensuring co-operation of all interested in the matter. The school prospectus or catalog should be written with a guidance viewpoint expressed.

One recommendation which is of utmost importance until all teachers have received training in vocational guidance is this: trained specialists in the field should not be diverted to other fields, not even to administrative work, unless such administrative duties will permit the continuance of work in guidance.

Religious Communities have the greatest need for sane, prudent vocational guidance to discover and utilize to the fullest possible extent the specific talents, either latent or developed, of the members.

All the activities suggested may seem to call for great expenditure of effort, but the choice of lifework is a momentous task for the individual and for society. All types of social workers testify continually to the baneful effects of occupational maladjustment, and on the contrary, to the constructive social contribution of developing in the student's mind (1) a knowledge of the world's work, (2) an interest in work and avocations of the student's choice, (3) a habit of industry, and (4) a sense of the happiness resulting from achievement in any constructive work; they urge the guidance of youth to the point of functioning interest as a preventive of crime and social waste. If we undertake to educate the youth, his needs must be met, and this is the field of greatest need in the age of adolescence.

EPILOGUE

THIS is an era of transition, of adjustment. The American people confidently look to education as the means for accomplishing effective transition and adjustment. Only by truly individualizing education, and spurring students to realize their maximum potentialities, can this confidence be maintained. But this education must consider "the whole aggregate of human life," physical, mental, moral, social, and spiritual, and in considering it, must accomplish effective change. Mass education cannot accomplish this change. The human being responds to the personal stimulus, depends upon human guidance for the interpretation of life with its many facets until he is able to take up for himself the search for truth. If we view guidance as synonymous with the educative process as it exists today, like a wave in water it will lose its force and almost its identity before the desired shore is reached.

Guidance to be effective must discover a core around which may be wrapped constructive and contributing habits. Choice of lifework offers this opportunity, an occasion for considering specific habits which contribute to the life of the adolescent, or habits which are desirable but not yet acquired. While making a life and making a living are not synonymous, successful adjustment to lifework is often the point of departure for a successful life, and the one rarely is found without the other.

Our science of life has fallen far short of requirements. Our achievements in technology have made us so proud that we do not realize we have failed at the point where failure is fatal—in not developing man, the master of science. A thoughtful educator warned us: "Education is a process, and the universal failure of educators is due to the fact that they think they must turn out products, whereas their task is to start, stimulate, and direct processes of self-activity that shall last as long as life." [92] This stimulating and directing, which is the integral part of student guidance, of necessity must be permeated with the thought expressed by a scientist of whom the world is proud: "Sci-

155

ence does not consist exclusively of the conquest of matter. Man is the most important. We are victims of the backwardness of the sciences of life over those of matter.

"Scientific research should be inspired today by the new ideal, the will to make man master of himself. There can be no other builder of man than himself, and to build a new civilization, imagination, intelligence, and moral strength of purpose are necessary.

"We must realize that the ultimate purpose of civilization is not the invention of machines and the progress of laboratory sciences, but the development of the human person. Neither science nor reason will ever lead mankind. But science is capable of helping us with three precious gifts—a knowledge of ourselves, the means to construct environment, and the power to build man endowed with a greater intelligence and spiritual virility. So science may have a more profound and solemn significance in the civilization of tomorrow than it has in the civilization of today." [93]

While Catholic secondary schools have a very great advantage in the devoted life-service of their teachers, in the personal contacts of these teachers with the students, possible because of the average smaller student bodies, and in the emphasis on the spiritual development of the students as a foundation for effective habits, too often their service has ended with the bare foundation. Vocational and educational guidance are an integral part of the project of building a life. Here Catholic schools have not fully realized their responsibility. Catholic secondary schools must assume their responsibility for offering this guidance, and so "build men with greater intelligence and spiritual virility." It is time for action!

APPENDIX

Benedictine Academy
840 North Broad Street
Elizabeth, New Jersey

Dear Friend:

Will you help me to disprove the charge that Catholic Schools will not answer questionnaires? I would like to disprove it by saying that I have had a 100% return on the check-list enclosed, forwarded promptly! I shall be able to report this 100% only if YOU check and forward promptly this list in the stamped, addressed envelope. Will you do it?

The form has been simplified so that it should not take more than three minutes to read and check it, while it is still fresh in your mind. I know from experience that it is more difficult to return to it, after laying it aside, so give me your first reaction—pen or pencil does not matter. Sign if you wish. NO NAMES OF SCHOOLS WILL BE USED.

It is not necessary to have student-guidance to answer this check-list. If you have no guidance activities at all, won't you just check questions 1, 2 and 3 and mail it? If, however, you have any of the activities listed, won't you check them so that you may be credited with them?

I do not expect to find much organized guidance, for there is only a minor percentage in public schools with their much more ample funds and personnel. Therefore, please do not think it a reflection on your school if you do not have student guidance, nor on our Catholic Schools as a body. What matters is— please do not be the one to spoil the 100%! "He gives twice who gives quickly."

Thank you for your cordial co-operation.

Gratefully yours,
SISTER TERESA GERTRUDE, O.S.B.

QUESTIONNAIRE OF VOCATIONAL AND EDUCATIONAL GUIDANCE

Names of Schools will not be used.

1. Are you interested in Vocational and Educational Guidance, i.e., choosing a life-work, not a religious vocation? Yes...... No......
2. How was your interest aroused in Guidance? through speakers...... through State Requirements...... through the Nat'l Catholic Educational Ass'n...... through your own reading...... through observing the need for guidance......

3. Do you provide vocational guidance for students in your school? Yes......
No......
4. In what year did you begin any work of this kind in your school?......
In what grade, or year of school did you begin?...... Why did you choose
this grade?......
5. Did you begin the work on an informal basis, i.e. by talking with students?...... or did you begin with an organized class, i.e. by instruction?......
6. Have you changed from the informal to the more organized form, i.e. in a
class for guidance?...... or studying occupations?...... or vocational
Civics?...... or English themes on the subject?......other classes? Which
ones?
7. Will you check any of the following you have used (please check twice
those you are now using) either as a means of giving information or as a
tryout of the student's abilities, capacities or interests:
Assembly talks by Representatives of Vo-
cations ....Clubs ....
Student interviews with Representatives
of Vocations ....Meetings after school....
Assembly talks by Teachers or School
Officers ....Class in Occupations....
Student interviews with Teachers or
School Officers ....Follow-up of Graduates..
Case studies of students' problems..............Follow-up of drop-outs..
Occupational observation and field-trips.........Physical examination....
Intelligence....Achievement...... Follow-up of: Bright students...
Tests: Aptitude...... Mechanical Ability.... Failing students..
Personnel Classification.......
Character study and practice.......
Referring students to vocational literature......
8. In beginning guidance did you use all teachers? Yes...... No...... Home-
room teachers Yes...... No...... Selected teachers Yes...... No......
9. Have you increased the time given to the subject? Yes...... No......
Why?......
10. Do you now offer a class in Occupations? Yes...... No...... When was
it begun?............ Is it a required subject? Yes...... No......How
much credit is given for it?.................
11. In what year of high school is it given? 1....2....3....4.... If you have
changed the year, when was it given previously? 1....2....3....4....
Why was the change made?.................
12. What texts are used?
If no texts, what reference books?
13. Does the Principal act as Counselor? Yes...... No......
14. Does any other School Officer act as Counselor? Yes......................
(NAME)
No......

15. Do you have a Counselor? Yes...... No...... More than one? Yes......
No...... What title is he given? ....
16. Does he give full time to Counseling duties?...... Yes...... No......
If he is part-time teacher, what subjects does he teach? ....
17. How much time does he give to Counselor's duties? ....
18. Was the Counselor a teacher who prepared for counseling? Yes......
No......
19. Has he had special training for counseling? Yes...... No...... Trained
"in service" by reading, study and experience? Yes...... No......
20. If specially trained, where did he receive training?..................
21. Is he a member of a Religious Order? Yes...... No...... or a Priest?
Yes...... No......
22. What relation does he have to Advisers for Classes, Deans, et al.? ....
23. Do students have individual interviews with the Counselor? Yes......
No...... Freshman...... Sophomore...... Junior...... Senior......
24. How many interviews usually in the student's high school life?............
25. Do you present a survey of all occupations in the class? Yes...... No......
only of local occupations? Yes...... No......
26. Have local occupations and employment been surveyed? Yes...... No......
When?............ by whom?.................. What agencies cooperated
in this survey? Chamber of Commerce? Yes...... No...... Other agencies?
27. Are reports of surveys made to the Counselor's office? Yes...... No......
How are they kept up-to-date? ....By whom? ....
28. Are guidance records of students kept? Yes...... No...... Are these
records centralized for use by Faculty? Yes...... No......
29. Do Counselors make placements of students, i.e. obtain positions or try-out
and practice work for students? Yes...... No......
30. Do Counselors follow-up the employed to see the success of the student in
the work or in that particular place of work? Yes...... No......
31. Are your Alumni organized to assist your students in guidance and field-
trips, also employment? Yes...... No......
32. Are students assisted in a choice of college or technical school? Yes......
No......
33. Do you assist your Alumni? Yes...... No......
34. What assistance can I give you in this work? I shall be pleased to do anything possible.

Signed ....
(POSITION?)

Thank you sincerely for your co-operation and time,

Sister Teresa Gertrude, O.S.B.
Benedictine Academy
840 N. Broad St., Elizabeth, N.J.

BIBLIOGRAPHY

Original Sources

Catholic Secondary School Reports, 1932.
Questionnaires on "The Catholic Central High School."
All completed research reviewed in Chapter III.
Superintendents' Reports, 1934.
Catalogs of Colleges and Universities.
Questionnaires on Guidance Practice in Present Investigation.
St. Benedict's "Rule."
Acta et Decreta Concilii Plenarii Baltimorensis Tertii, 1886.
Acta et Decreta Conciliorum Provincialium, Cincinnatensium, 1855, 1882, 1886.

Periodicals

National Catholic Education Association, Bulletins and Proceedings, 1899–1936.
Official Catholic Directory.
Directory of Catholic Schools and Colleges, 1932–1933, and Pamphlet Series, 1935–1936.
Yearbooks of National Education Association, Department of Secondary Schools.
Yearbooks of National Society for the Study of Education.
Proceedings of Franciscan and Benedictine Educational Conferences.

General*

1. White House Conference Report. Education and Training—Subcommittee on Vocational Guidance. The Century Company, New York, 1932.
2. National Catholic Education Association. Proceedings 1904, Committee on High Schools.
3. Kitson, H. D. How to Find the Right Vocation. Harper and Brothers, New York, 1929, pp. 81–83.
4. National Catholic Education Association, Proceedings, 1905, p. 50.
5. National Catholic Education Association, Proceedings, 1905, p. 65.
6. National Catholic Education Association, Proceedings, 1905, p. 75.
7. National Catholic Education Association, Proceedings, 1906, p. 182.
8. National Catholic Education Association, Proceedings, 1906, p. 195.
9. National Catholic Education Association, Proceedings, 1906, p. 201.
10. National Catholic Education Association, Proceedings, 1907, p. 178.
11. National Catholic Education Association, Proceedings, 1907, p. 184.

* The following references are referred to by number in the text.

12. National Catholic Education Association, Proceedings, 1907, p. 190.
13. Report from Philadelphia Archdiocese, 1932. Superintendent of Schools.
14. National Catholic Education Association, Proceedings, 1910, p. 243.
15. National Catholic Education Association, Proceedings, 1911, pp. 61 ff.
16. National Catholic Education Association, Proceedings, 1911, p. 112.
17. National Catholic Education Association, Proceedings, 1911, p. 296.
18. National Catholic Education Association, Proceedings, 1911, pp. 306 ff.
19. National Catholic Education Association, Proceedings, 1912, p. 238.
20. National Catholic Education Association, Proceedings, 1912, p. 267.
21. National Catholic Education Association, Proceedings, 1912, p. 301.
22. National Catholic Education Association, Proceedings, 1912, p. 307.
23. National Catholic Education Association, Proceedings, 1914, pp. 158 ff.
24. National Catholic Education Association, Proceedings, 1915, p. 312.
25. National Catholic Education Association, Proceedings, 1915, pp. 337, 444.
26. National Catholic Education Association, Proceedings, 1917, pp. 241, 239, 476.
27. National Catholic Education Association, Proceedings, 1917, p. 97.
28. National Catholic Education Association, Proceedings, 1917, p. 239.
29. National Catholic Education Association, Proceedings, 1917, p. 245.
30. National Catholic Education Association, Proceedings, 1917, p. 229.
31. Sister M. Jeannette (Roesch), O.S.B., Ph.D., Dissertation, Catholic University of America, 1918.
32. National Catholic Education Association, Proceedings, 1918, p. 282.
33. National Catholic Education Association, Proceedings, 1918, p. 496.
34. National Catholic Education Association, Proceedings, 1918, p. 334.
35. National Catholic Education Association, Proceedings, 1918, p. 350.
36. National Catholic Education Association, Proceedings, 1918, p. 528.
37. National Catholic Education Association, Proceedings, 1918, p. 573.
38. New Orleans, La., Report of Guidance Activities, 1932.
39. National Catholic Education Association, Proceedings, 1919, p. 363.
40. National Catholic Education Association, Proceedings, 1919, pp. 279 ff.
41. National Catholic Education Association, Proceedings, 1920, pp. 271, 373, 485.
42. National Catholic Education Association, Proceedings, 1921, pp. 301, 198, 237, 245.
43. National Catholic Education Association, Proceedings, 1922, pp. 267, 282, 308.
44. National Catholic Education Association, Proceedings, 1923, pp. 201, 221.
45. National Catholic Education Association, Proceedings, 1924, pp. 570, 582, 602.
46. National Catholic Education Association, Proceedings, 1924, pp. 382, 145.
47. National Catholic Education Association, Proceedings, 1924, pp. 281, 328, 510.
48. National Catholic Education Association, Proceedings, 1924, pp. 238, 341, 529.
49. National Catholic Education Association, Proceedings, 1925, p. 149.
50. National Catholic Education Association, Proceedings, 1930, pp. 320-339.
51. National Catholic Education Association, Proceedings, 1931, pp. 373-440.
52. National Catholic Education Association, Proceedings, 1932, pp. 212-350.

53. National Catholic Education Association, Proceedings, 1933, pp. 229–326.

54. National Catholic Education Association, Proceedings, 1934, p. 206.

55. National Catholic Education Association, Proceedings, 1935, pp. 111–115; 202–256.

56. National Catholic Education Association, Proceedings, 1936, pp. 314; 233.

57. Encyclical Letter of Pope Pius XI on "The Christian Priesthood," National Catholic Welfare Conference. Washington, D. C.

58. Wolff, Bernice L. The Sodality Movement in the United States, 1926–1936, Unpublished Master's Thesis in files of St. Louis University, 1936.

59. Milwaukee Archdiocesan Report on Vocational Guidance.

60. Catholic School Journal. Bruce Co., Milwaukee, Wis., March, 1930.

61. Ryan, Rev. Carl J., Ph.D. The Central Catholic High School. Catholic University, 1927.

62. Chouinard, Rev. Anthony J., A.M. Extracurricular Activities in Catholic High Schools, Unpublished Master's Thesis in files of Catholic University, Washington, D. C., 1927.

63. Hagan, Rev. John R., Ph.D., Ed.D. Catholic Teachers' Colleges. Catholic University, 1927.

64. O'Neill, Bro. Francis de Sales, Ph.D. (F.S.C.). The Catholic High School Curriculum. Catholic University of America, 1930.

65. Rooney, Rev. John R., Ph.D. Curricular Offerings in 283 Catholic High Schools, Catholic Education Press, Washington, D. C., 1931.

66. Sister M. Clarence (Friesenhahn), Div. Prov., Ph.D. Curricular Offerings of Secondary Schools of the Province of San Antonio, Texas. Catholic University, Washington, D. C., 1930.

67. McGuire, Rev. William P. A., Ph.D. Brooklyn Diocesan Curricular Offerings in High Schools. Catholic University of America, Washington, D. C., 1932.

68. Koos, Leonard V., Ph.D. Private and Public Secondary Education in Minnesota. University of Chicago Press, Chicago, 1931.

69. Crowley, Francis J., Ph.D. The Catholic High School Principal. Bruce Co., Milwaukee, 1934.

70. McGucken, Rev. Wm. J., S.J., Ph.D. Jesuit Secondary Education. Bruce Co., Milwaukee, 1932.

71. Sister M. Mildred (Knoebber), O.S.B., Ph.D. The Self-Revelations of the Adolescent Girl. Bruce Co., Milwaukee, 1937.

72. Sister M. Clarice (Gansirt), O.P., Ph.D. The Status of Vocational Guidance in 274 Large Catholic High Schools. Notre Dame University, Indiana, 1933.

73. Sister M. Priscilla (Freidel), Notre Dame, Ph.D. Guidance Practices in 50 Catholic High Schools. Fordham University, New York, 1933.

74. Sister M. Ignata (Biehn), S.C.C., Ph.D. Vocational Practices in Girls' High Schools in Nine Midwestern States. Loyola University, Chicago, 1933.

75. Sister M. Irmina (Kelly), I.H.M., A.M. A Study of Vocational Guidance

in Girls' High Schools in Philadelphia, Pennsylvania. Villanova College, 1933.

76. Acta et Decreta Conciliorum Provincialium, Cincinnatensium, 1855 to 1882. Benziger Bros., Cincinnati, 1886.

77. Acta et Decreta Concilii Plenarii Baltimorensis Tertii. J. Murphy, Baltimore, 1886.

78. Voelker, Rev. John, Ph.D. The Diocesan Superintendent of Schools. Catholic University of America, Washington, D. C., 1935.

79. Burns, Rev. J. A., C.S.C., Ph.D. (a) Principles, Origin and Establishment of the Catholic School System, 1908. (b) Growth and Development of the Catholic School System, 1912. (c) Catholic Education, 1917. Benziger Bros., New York.

80. Official Catholic Directory. Issued annually by P. J. Kennedy and Sons, New York.

81. National Catholic Welfare Conference, Department of Education. Directory of Catholic Schools and Colleges, 1932–33; pamphlets, 1935–36. Washington, D. C.

82. Department of the Interior, Office of Education. Biennial Survey of Education in the United States, 1928–30, 1932. Washington, D. C.

83. Department of the Interior, Office of Education. Accredited Secondary Schools of the United States, Bulletin 1934, No. 17. Washington, D. C.

84. O'Dowd, Rev. J. T., Ph.D. Effects of Accreditation on Catholic Secondary Schools. Catholic University of America, Washington, D. C., 1935.

85. Crowley, Dr. Francis J. Remarkable Growth of Catholic Secondary Schools. School Life, Vol. 14, pp. 112–14, February, 1929. Washington, D. C.

86. Cooper, Rev. John M., Ph.D. Religion Outlines for College, Book IV. Catholic Education Press. Washington, D. C., 1932.

87. National Catholic Education Association, Proceedings, 1931, p. 392.

88. Butler, Pres. Nicholas Murray, Ph.D. The Meaning of Education, p. 151. Macmillan Co., 1898.

89. Encyclical Letter on Christian Education of Youth, Pope Pius XI. Edition issued by National Catholic Welfare Conference, p. 36. Washington, D. C., 1930.

90. Hurlin, Ralph G. Occupational Census of Catholic Sisterhoods in the United States. Russell Sage Foundation, New York, 1933.

91. Encyclical Letter on Christian Priesthood, Pope Pius XI. National Catholic Welfare Conference, Washington, D. C., 1936.

92. Spalding, Archbishop J. L. Glimpses of Truth. McClurg and Co., Chicago, 1903.

93. Carrel, Dr. Alexis. Quoted in National Catholic Education Association Proceedings, 1936, p. 93. From Address at the University of Southern California, March, 1936.

VITA

Sister M. Teresa Gertrude, of the Order of St. Benedict.

Motherhouse: Elizabeth, New Jersey.

Born: Dubuque, Iowa, December 3, 1884.

Educated: Dubuque High School, 1903.
   Iowa State Teacher's College, Bachelor of Didactics, 1906.
   University of Chicago, Bachelor of Arts, 1910.
   Fordham University, Master of Arts, 1930.

Experience: Teacher and Principal of High Schools (Public) 1906–1917.
   Iowa and Nebraska.
   Educational Director in Department Stores, Chicago and Baltimore,
   1918-1920.
   Training Officer, Federal Board for Vocational Education, Rehabili-
   tation Division, Washington, D. C., 1920-1921.
   Training Officer, U. S. Veterans' Bureau, Washington, D. C.,
   1921–1926.
   Executive Secretary, Diocesan Council of Catholic Women, Newark,
   New Jersey, 1926–1927.

Honor Society: Kappa Delta Pi, Kappa Chapter.

Listed in: American Women.